TEACHING TRANSFERENCE
On the Foundations of Psychoanalytic Studies

Edited by
MARTIN STANTON & DAVID REASON

Rebus Press
London

First published 1996
by Rebus Press Ltd
1c High Street
LONDON SW13 9LB

© 1996 Martin Stanton and David Reason

Made in the United Kingdom

All rights reserved. No part of this book may be reprinted or reproduced or utilized in any form or by any electronic, mechanical, or by other means, now known or hereafter invented, including photocopying and recording, or in any information strorage and retrieval system, without permission in writing from the publishers.

ISBN 1 900877 01 5

Contents

Introduction   1
Martin Stanton and David Reason

PSYCHOANALYSIS AND THE ACADEMIC DISCIPLINES

The Future of Psychoanalytic Studies   9
Martin Stanton

The Future of Jungian Studies   15
Andrew Samuels

Teaching and Psychoanalysis: A Necessary Impossiblity   27
Paul Verhaeghe

Thinking Psychoanalytically in the University   44
Karl Figlio

The Crisis of Univers(al)ity and the Future of Psychoanalytic Studies   59
Attila Banfalvi

Psychoanalysis, Psychoanalytic Studies and Universities   69
Alison Hall

THINKING PSYCHOANALYTICALLY

Finding an Ear: Reflections on an Analytic Journey   79
Gerald Gargiulo

Some Assertions about Self   90
Joel Ryce-Menuhin

The Structural Problem in Phobia　　　　　　　　98
Bernard Burgoyne

Imagos and the Problem of the Imaginary　　　114
Martin Stanton

Letters and Symptoms: Lacan and Literature　　125
Luke Thurston

A Sound Idea　　　　　　　　　　　　　　　135
Rosemary Dunn

Genealogy of the Museum: John Bargrave's Cabinet in　145
Context
Stephen Bann

Racism, Incest and Modernity: Everyone is now a　139
Stranger among Strangers
Christopher Hauke

From the Pleasure of Power to the Power of Pleasure:　184
Popular Culture in Search of a New Identity
Milena Kirova

Index　　　　　　　　　　　　　　　　　　190

Contributors

Attila Banfalvi is a lecturer in Psychoanalysis in the Department of Medicine at the University of Debrecen in Hungary.

Stephen Bann is Professor of Modern Cultural Studies in the School of Arts and Image Studies at the University of Kent

Bernard Burgoyne is Director of the Centre for Psychoanalytic Studies at Middlesex University and a founder member of the Centre for Freudian Analysis and Research (CFAR).

Rosemary Dunn is a doctoral student at the Centre for Psychoanalytic Studies at the University of Kent

Karl Figlio is Director of the Centre for Psychoanalytic Studies at the University of Essex, and a member of the Association of Group and Individual Psychotherapy (AGIP).

Gerald Gargiulo is Director of the National Psychological Association for Psychoanalysis (NPAP) in New York, and President of the International Federation for Psychoanalytic Education (IFPE).

Alison Hall is Director of Psychoanalytic Studies in the School of Cultural Studies at Leeds Metropolitan University, and Chair of the Universities Association for Psychoanalytic Studies (UAPS)

Christopher Hauke is Chair of the Greenwich Consortium of Psychotherapists, a member of the Society of Analytical Psychology (SAP) in London and a lecturer in Psychoanalytic Studies at the University of Kent and Goldsmiths College, London.

Milena Kirova is a lecturer in the Department of Bulgarian Literature at the University of Sofia in Bulgaria.

David Reason is Director of Research at the Centre for Psychoanalytic Studies at the University of Kent.

Joel Ryce-Menuhin is a training analyst and supervisor at the Independent Group of Analytical Psychologists and the Founding Director of the British and Irish Sandplay Assocication.

Andrew Samuels is Professor of Analytical Psychology at the University of Essex, and a training analyst at the Society of Analytical Psychology (SAP) in London

Martin Stanton is Director of the Centre for Psychoanalytic Studies at the University of Kent, and a Council Member of the London Centre for Psychotherapy (LCP).

Luke Thurston is a doctoral student at the Centre for Psychoanalytic Studies at the University of Kent

Paul Verhaeghe is Professor of Psychoanalysis in the Department of Psychology at the University of Ghent in Belgium

Introduction
Martin Stanton & David Reason

When the University of Kent launched the first degree in Psychoanalytic Studies in 1985, and the first Centre for Psychoanalytic Studies in 1986, the British academic world was sceptical about its chances of survival. Even two years later, after the new MA in Psychoanalytic Studies had actually survived and even recruited a healthy number of students, Brian Morton wittily entitled his feature on the Kent programme, 'Dream Degree'.[1] It was a 'dream' in the double sense of trying to incorporate in its own right the psychoanalytic study of unconscious process (pioneered by Freud in The Interpretation of Dreams), and in its ambition to realise an intentionally unreal 'dream', for such a new and interdisciplinary programme was widely perceived as running counter to the then current British government policy of stringently cutting back the university sector to its well-established roots. 'Completion rates on the Freudian couch', Morton quipped, 'are well below Swinnerton-Dyer-preferred averages.' (Swinnerton-Dyer was then Chair of the Universities Funding Council).

Despite this founding air of 'unreality', both the Centre for Psychoanalytic Studies, and the associated MA in Psychoanalytic Studies, grew rapidly in their first five years as sole exemplars of the new species. Student application was considerably greater than the available teaching resourcing, so a quota had to be imposed on student recruitment; conferences and study days covered a broad spectrum of themes and schools, and consequently attracted a wide range of support; the policy of negotiating academic research exchanges with East and West European, North American and Australian colleagues generated a foreign staff and student presence that immeasurably enriched the growing graduate research community; and, finally, many new and experienced clinical practitioners of psychoanalysis and psychoanalytic psychotherapy gave full and enthusiastic support, either through enrolling for research degrees, through giving guest lectures and seminars, or through

---

[1] Times Higher Education Supplement, 12 February 1988.

donating books and archival sources. The Centre and its academic programmes rapidly established a reputation for an interdisciplinary approach which refused to 'privilege' either clinical or academic frameworks in the development of Psychoanalytic Studies; we rather sought to put the relationship between these two spheres continually in question. We encouraged a vigorous and invigorating breadth of interest among our students and visitors (and, vigilantly, ourselves and our colleagues), and were so successful that, as often as not, Kleinians believed us Jungian, Jungians considered us among the Freudian faithful, and everyone who was anyone else was convinced that - having clearly 'mastered' the Fourth Discourse - we were enrolled in a Lacanian Fifth Column. Of course, all persuasions found a welcome, albeit that the hospitality was and is offered in a spirit of constructive and collegial criticism.

Since 1990, Psychoanalytic Studies in Britain has been fundamentally transformed through the introduction of a number of new courses, all of which inevitably related in some way (albeit marginally or differentially) to the 'Kent model'. We would note, in chronological order, the Universities of Middlesex, Brunel, Leeds Metropolitan, East London, Sheffield, LSB Dublin, Trinity Dublin, Hertfordshire, Belfast, Manchester, Goldsmiths' London, Essex, Bristol, and University College, London.

> The very coexistence of these courses has posed practical questions about the common foundations, aims, and objectives of Psychoanalytic Studies as a university subject; questions like: what does it mean to 'think psychoanalytically'?
>
> What differentiates thinking psychoanalytically from other forms of thought?
>
> Is there any academic obligation, following the Kent model, for Psychoanalytic Studies to be eclectic, and therefore open to all critical (including negative critical) approaches?
>
> What place and what importance should be given to clinical work and perspectives in Psychoanalytic Studies?

Introduction

Should there be some obligatory clinical experience (personal analysis, registered psychotherapist status, or experiential group experience) in university Psychoanalytic Studies programmes?

Each of the courses listed above has generated its own specific response to these questions, some of which will be covered in detail in contributions to this volume. In addition, there are now two national research bodies, The Higher Education Research and Information Network in Psychoanalysis (THERIP), and The Universities Association for Psychoanalytic Studies (UAPS), which aim to address differences of approach, and related issues of research co-operation in the field. THERIP aims to promote general public discussion, research, and information in psychoanalysis broadly conceived; and UAPS is exclusively concerned with Psychoanalytic Studies as a university subject. Both these organisations have had an important impact on the way in which clinicians, academics, and indeed the general public perceive this general field. In particular, they have drawn attention to the need for debate and discussion across the various psychoanalytic schools of thought, and also clearly indicated the importance of introducing research into both the clinical and applied fields.

What constitutes a proper background for Psychoanalytic Studies? Most if not all courses currently on offer follow the Kent design of two core courses which cover the history and development of the psychoanalytic movement, and survey the major psychoanalytic concepts. These core courses are then supplemented by a choice of specialist option courses. A main reason for this design has been the absence of any undergraduate programme in Psychoanalytic Studies, which has obliged the MA programmes to assume no prior knowledge before starting the course. This situation is presently changing rapidly. The introduction of undergraduate degree programmes in Psychoanalytic Studies at LSB College, Dublin (1994), and Leeds Metropolitan (1996) will undoubtedly inaugurate a new long-term trend, which will in turn inevitably impact on the conception of post-graduate Psychoanalytic Studies programmes. If the provision of background knowledge is located firmly in undergraduate programmes, then post-graduate courses could well move towards a greater degree of research-led specialisation in individual courses. This move towards specialisation would also in turn transform the conception of 'background' to the subject - not least because any background course would have to integrate new research-led material.

At some point in the future pedagogical development of Psychoanalytic Studies, then, individual courses will be forced to pool their efforts and negotiate formal co-operative structures. An important priority here must be the establishment of a consolidated network of credit transfer agreements to facilitate student choice and mobility. This network will not only cover the university world, but also psychoanalytic trainings in the private sector, whose range of clinical expertise and training is not generally available in universities. In this context, the Centre for Psychoanalytic Studies at the University of Kent pioneered the first credit transfer agreement with the clinical training of the London Centre for Psychotherapy in 1993, which facilitated the interchange of students between clinical and research options.

As a new university subject with a special relationship with the clinical world, Psychoanalytic Studies seems destined to pass through a period of fluidity in which numerous options will be tried and tested. In this situation it is particularly important to hold on to the basic issues that provoked the foundation of the subject in the first place. Central here is the issue of the character of psychoanalytic thinking - and we use the term 'character' fully mindful of its use by Abraham, Ferenczi, Reich and others to indicate all that is rigid and automatic about human behaviour. One of the great challenges posed by the participation of Psychoanalytic Studies in university life is precisely that it is obliged to negotiate other modes of thought and argument, and indeed subject its own modus operandi to stringent critique.

Today, three prominent and distinctive critical concerns characterise psychoanalytic thinking. First, there is a primary concern to distinguish the unconscious structure in all material for study - which leads to ever increasing refinement of critical tools to uncover unconscious process and render it accessible. Secondly, the concern for different forms of narrative process - particularly how people fail to express themselves, or express what they did not mean - and the inevitable temporal issues (the befores-and-afters of narratives) that impose themselves. Thirdly, there is an increasing awareness of the cultural situation of psychoanalytic theory and practice, an awareness honed on the momentous social, economic

Introduction

and political transformations we are witnessing as we approach the millenium. We are still very far from understanding the nature of the enmeshment of even the core psychoanalytic concepts and precepts in the wider historical process, nor how exactly psyche is geared to our present-day highly mediated sociality.

These critical concerns run throughout the contributions to this book, and are approached and processed in different ways. The first section focuses on the variety of issues raised by the presence of Psychoanalytic Studies in universities. The second section freely ranges over the diversity of teaching and research interests that have developed within the subject. The contributors to this modest volume are all associated with the Centre for Psychoanalytic Studies at the University of Kent at Canterbury - teachers and clinicians and students from the United Kingdom and abroad - and in these writings, individually and collectively, they come together as members not of a discipline but of a community of Psychoanalytic Studies, to 'think psychoanalytically' (in their variety of ways and fashions) and to celebrate the future potential of this field and subject of thought and practice. The book serves, therefore, both as a guide-book to a new area of university life, and as a celebration of a decade of 'living' it. In important ways, the presence of Psychoanalytic Studies in universities has allowed psychoanalysis different interdisciplinary contexts in which to discover its potential to relate to current research, seemingly strange methodologies, and other perspectives on the human condition. With luck and commitment, neither the universities nor psychoanalysis will be untouched, unmarked, unmoved by the experience, and, in another decade, in that looming millenium, will remark that notable dialectic with a fittingly 'unbuttoned' celebration.

PSYCHOANALYSIS AND THE ACADEMIC DISCIPLINES

The Future of Psychoanalytic Studies
Martin Stanton

Since its inception as a university subject ten years ago, Psychoanalytic Studies has developed from precarious infancy towards flamboyant pre-teenagehood. It presently attracts substantially more students in UK and Irish universities than university Psychotherapy courses, and there is a current flourish in the establishment of new undergraduate as well as postgraduate degree programmes. Besides generating income from the private sector in an era of declining government funding, this visible and much-publicised growth has also provoked increasing alarm amongst some clinicians. They are concerned above all about the general effects of teaching Psychoanalytic Studies without an obligatory clinical component; effects that will be substantially amplified by the future large numbers of Psychoanalytic Studies graduates who will consider themselves 'experts' in this field. Furthermore, the relatively small number of psychoanalysts who invest large sums of private income in their clinical training will be vastly outnumbered by potentially grant-maintained non-clinical graduates. The main fear here is that the boundaries between clinical and applied psychoanalysis will be increasingly infringed and ultimately collapse, thus divesting the clinical practice of psychoanalysis of any vestige of respectability.[1]

To some extent, such fear is fuelled by inevitable transformations in the general mental health field, in which classical psychoanalysis (five sessions a week for at least four years) has a minimal clinical future. In the United States, psychoanalysts have been forced dras-

---

[1] Stanton, Martin (1995), 'The False Dichotomy between Clinical and Applied Psychoanalysis', in The Future of Psychoanalytic Education, ed. Stephen Friedlander, American Psychological Association, 1995. For a comparative view, see Adams, Michael (1994), 'Psychoanalytic Studies in British and American Universities: the Kent and New School Programs', IFPE Journal, vol. 3, pt. 1, Spring 1994.

tically to modify their conceptions of both clinical practice and training, and reduce accordingly their requirements simply to remain financially viable. Furthermore, medical and psychiatric units recommend classic psychoanalytic treatment for a diminishing number of mental disorders, principally because other forms of psychotherapy (including psychoanalytic psychotherapy) have rated much higher in outcome research. Under these circumstances, medical insurance companies are now generally unwilling to cover the cost of such treatment.

It would be misguided to attribute these changes exclusively to financial pressures, or indeed to suggest that this decline in clinical referrals heralds the 'end' of psychoanalysis. It is important rather to study such transformations in the context of important shifting public demands and expectations of psychoanalysis. First of all, there has been a perceptible de-pathologization of general psychoanalytic psychotherapy and counselling: the social stigmatisation associated with visiting a therapist or counsellor has significantly decreased, and there is now general recognition that it is 'normal' for people suffering from trauma, bereavement, relationship problems, and stress, to consider therapy. Secondly, the central concern with 'cure' - along with its problematic relationship to medical intervention - has been diverted away from classical psychoanalysis in the direction of treatment programmes designed for specific disorders (such as phobias, PTSD, eating disorders, dissociative disorders, etc.). These programmes are generally combinatory, often involving both psychopharmacological and psychotherapeutic input, and certainly have no anti-psychoanalytic intent. Unlike classical psychoanalysis, they do not engage with general issues relating to psychic process, but rather address directly (if sometimes narrowly) the specific presenting symptoms of a given disorder, and utilise all appropriate available methods to address them.

Such clinical specialisation has perhaps enabled the new development of a general educational potential in psychoanalysis. The prodigious growth of Psychoanalytic Studies may well indicate a relative shift of emphasis from psychoanalytic cure towards psychoanalytic education. Psychoanalytic education here evokes the classical sense of ex-ducare (to draw out): to draw out the unconscious structuring of blind spot and fantasy intrusion that disrupts relationships, or dislocates the sense of self and other, or infringes the fragile boundary between inner and outer world. In these senses, psychoanalytic education is not separate from the clinical, but simply removed from exclusively curative clinical preoccupations. There is no 'educative' replacement for clinical work, and no amount of study can substitute for personal analysis. Unfortunately, some students do indeed turn to Psychoanalytic Studies courses to substitute for personal analysis, and the resultant effect on the group can be extremely destructive. Likewise, some teachers - even supposedly extensively analysed ones - can destructively destabilise the educative process through the intrusion of unconscious material which belongs more to their personal analysis than to the classroom or lecture theatre. Clearly, these situations give rise to serious cause for concern - a concern which undoubtedly underpins some of the general fears about Psychoanalytic Studies mentioned earlier.

Obviously, such concern might be considerably alleviated if there were indeed a formal level of clinical support, to which such problems might be relayed: at Kent, as elsewhere, personal analysis is strongly recommended, and we are still trying to establish voluntary, non-assessed experiential groups, but the residual problem here is that current academic procedures preclude any obligatory commitment in these areas. Understandably, it is considered central to academic freedom and critical distance that a student be allowed to study a subject without 'believing' in it, or being 'committed' to it.[2] Conversely, to follow a vocational and pragmatic parallel, it would seem strange to allow someone to study French without building some performative and experiential element into the programme. In this context, the 'educative' impulse of Psychoanalytic Studies needs some complementary 'clinical' relay. Some indeed argue that this must be selective - not least because many students and teachers on Psychoanalytic Studies courses are extensively analysed and senior clinical practitioners - but this (like much 'classical' psychoanalysis) ignores the group level of the 'educational' process. In an essential way, psychoanalytic 'education' must utilise its own discoveries to distinguish itself from other subjects' *modi operandi*. In this context, students in Psychoanalytic Studies courses might be offered regular experiential groups, if only to confront and perhaps partially process the un-

---

[2] Stanton, M. (1990), 'Psychoanalysis in British Universities: the Kent Case', *Free Associations*, no 20.

conscious group levels of the formal 'educative' process. It would equally be a great and exciting challenge to devise ways in which such experiential work might be integrated into staff and student appraisal of personal and group achievement in the course.

Hopefully, the careful design of levels of clinical integration into Psychoanalytic Studies courses will enable specific 'educative' innovations to develop further, and become less controversial. Foremost here are the interdisciplinary developments promoted in the university context, and the integration of research perspectives into psychoanalytic work in general. Unfortunately, some Psychoanalytic Studies courses have abandoned broad critical study of the whole field and related subjects, and moved towards narrow and specific specialisations; they present themselves, for example, as British Object Relations courses, or Lacanian courses. Similarly, some have installed a registered clinical training as a prerequisite for entering the Psychoanalytic Studies course. The problem here is not the existence of such different sorts of course within the broad field of Psychoanalytic Studies - indeed let a thousand flowers bloom! - rather that this trend risks provoking a damaging false dichotomy between so-called 'orthodox' or clinically 'respectable' courses, and so-called 'radical' or eclectic ones. On the orthodox side of the false dichotomy, courses may be inevitably drawn to replicate the main monolithic features of 'classic' psychoanalytic training; and critical exegesis and study of the broad field will be eroded by singular focus on an exclusive psychoanalytic school. On the radical side of the false dichotomy, courses may well reactively respond by distancing, if not totally isolating themselves from psychoanalytic clinical work and clinical training.

These tendencies may be countered by thorough research of the complex needs placed on Psychoanalytic Studies by both the clinical and the academic world. From our experience at Kent, it seems clear that very different expectations are placed on Psychoanalytic Studies programmes. Some students look to the MA in Psychoanalytic Studies as an 'introductory' course to enable them to decide what sort of clinical training they wish to pursue; some are already registered psychotherapists, and look to the course as a 'post-graduate' supplement to clinical training which will enable them to proceed to doctoral research; finally, others look to the course as a means of acquiring mastery of psychoanalytic theory which they can then apply in a different area of research, such as art, film, literature, philosophy, or religious studies. In this context, it is not sufficient simply to note that these varied needs might prove ultimately incompatible - or generative of specific group conflict - but it is also important to consider how the very structure of Psychoanalytic Studies courses might be modified creatively to incorporate these differences.

A crucial factor here is the emergence of undergraduate degree programmes in Psychoanalytic Studies at LSB College Dublin and Leeds Metropolitan University. The fact that broad introductory courses in the history, theory, and practice of psychoanalysis will be increasingly available at undergraduate level, will undoubtedly provoke profound changes in the syllabi of postgraduate courses in the subject. A particular advantage here could be the removal of pressure on coursework MAs to be exhaustive, comprehensive, or indeed introductory. This advantage can be developed either through increasing the proportion of specialist options to core courses within the MA framework - and here a modular and credit transfer system could readily proliferate national and international combined programmes in Psychoanalytic Studies; or it could be developed through the design of short-term specialist courses to meet specific clinical training and academic research needs.[3] It would be possible, for example, to design a short-term course (1-3 terms part-time) on trauma for psychotherapists and mental health professionals; or a short-term course on trans-sexualism for psychotherapists and students from a range of other subjects such as Gender Studies, Sociology, Social Anthropology, and Social Work. A great advantage of such courses would be that they combine the acquisition of specific skills (such as psychoanalytic approaches to work with trauma-survivors or transsexuals) with specific research possibilities (such as qualitative studies of clinical assessment and treatment of disorders relating to these subjects).

In the future, therefore, it is likely that more opportunity for research will be incorporated both within Psychoanalytic Studies, and within clinical trainings, if effective modular transfer programmes are established. This could have a vital impact on clinical work in psychoanalysis, not least in providing a supplementary di-

---

[3] See in this connection Stanton, Martin (1993), 'The Role of Psychoanalytic Studies in Psychotherapy Training', British Journal of Psychotherapy, vol. 9, no 5, Winter 1993.

mension to reflect on the psychotherapeutic process. Two main areas of development seem likely here. First of all, the integration of specialist research skills into psychotherapeutic assessment: new research, for example, into the distinction between delusional and 'bizarre thought' material in Post-Traumatic Stress Disorder, which will enable clearer diagnostic differentiation of long-term and short-term features of the disorder; and finally, computer-assisted research methods which will enable more sophisticated methods of processing clinical material, and provide more accurate assessment of outcome.

The Future of Jungian Studies: A Personal Agenda

Andrew Samuels

Introduction

I will begin by surveying the situation of Studies in Analytical Psychology (sometimes referred to as Jungian Studies) in universities in this country and abroad. Then I will outline some of the difficulties that seem to exist in establishing analytical psychology as an area of knowledge and practice that should be engaged with at university level. Out of my experience of some of these difficulties, I think I can see a way to map or sketch out the various possibilities for teaching and research that exist in the area. I will cite my own efforts in relation to each part of the map and indicate those research interests that I should like to pursue.

Analytical Psychology and Psychoanalytic Studies

At present there are approximately twenty British universities offering degrees in 'psychoanalytic studies', 'psychotherapeutic studies', or 'psychotherapy'. Some of these degrees are non-clinical; others are clinical qualifications; a few attempt a combination or offer the student the choice of clinical or non-clinical routes to the degree. An informal questionnaire that I conducted recently concerning the non-clinical degree courses (mostly in psychoanalytic studies) suggests that there is not yet much attention paid to analytical psychology and virtually none at all to post-Jungian developments within analytical psychology. Probably the same applies to the clinical degree courses. An analogous situation would be if psychoanalytic studies were to ignore everything that has happened in psychoanalysis since Freud's death in 1939. Where Jung's texts are studied, it is invariably in terms of the break with Freud and as part of a process of schism within the early psychoanalytic movement up to 1913.

Apart from the recent establishment of the two joint Professorships at the University of Essex (funded by the Society of Analytical Psychology), the exception to the pattern of sidelining analytical psychology has been the Centre for Psychoanalytic Studies at the University of Kent. The Kent Centre has presented Jung Studies Days since 1990 and analytical psychology is now offered as an elective course. It is perhaps significant for the future of the Chair at Essex that in 1995 more of the MA students at Kent opted for the elective in post-Jungian analytical psychology than for similar electives focusing on Klein or Lacan (or, in fact, than for any other elective). The teaching is now being carried out by members of the Society of Analytical Psychology, including myself.

It is also worth recording that many of the university centres mentioned above are receiving numerous requests to undertake doctoral-level work in the general field of analytical psychology, to judge from the number of requests that my colleagues and I receive to supervise or examine these PhDs. There seems to be a groundswell of interest (some of it coming from abroad) from which the projects at Essex and Kent can benefit. When I first suggested in 1989-90 that the Society of Analytical Psychology should apply its legacy to the funding of a university appointment, I did not anticipate the fact that in 1995 some universities would be complaining that they did not have the resources to deal with doctoral-level interest in analytical psychology!

Analytical Psychology in the University: Difficulties and Possibilities

Over the past eight years, I have been offering to a number of universities a day-long event which focuses on Jungian and post-Jungian studies. One central feature has been a discussion of the problems associated with analytical psychology in the academy. We have tried to address these problems together with a critical-historical focus on some central theoretical concepts of analytical psychology. This leads on to a presentation of clinical and non-clinical themes from a post-Jungian perspective.

By now, I have conducted such day-long events, or given lectures, seminars and workshops, or participated in conferences on analytical psychology in this country or abroad in numerous universities. In my lectures, I ask the students to do a simple word association exercise to the word 'Jung' and the results have been instructive. I have obtained associations from over 300 students. The two associations that stand out (by overwhelming margins) are 'Freud' and 'anti-semitism/Nazism' (or something similar to those words). Third on the list we find 'mysticism/occult' or related words. These findings graphically illustrate the understandable background to the fact that, as the academic psychologist Liam Hudson put it, Jung has been 'comprehensively banished' from the university scene.

At the same time, judging by the degree of interest shown and the size of audiences at events that are not mandatory, the students, at all levels, are evincing considerable interest in analytical psychology and its ideas and practices. Hence, whilst not overlooking the biographical data we have on Jung which certainly informs many of his more central concepts, I have attempted to focus study on the social and cultural location of analytical psychology, its relation to psychoanalysis, its challenge to established epistemologies, and its utility (or lack of it) in applied forms in fields such as the human or social sciences, the arts generally, and religious studies.

Ambivalence concerning the name of 'Jung' coupled with an increasing interest in the Jungian traditions has also characterised clinical psychotherapeutic interest in analytical psychology. It is striking how many recognised psychotherapy trainings continue to offer a 'track' in analytical psychology at a time when theoretical hegemonies are being established that would seem to rule out analytical psychology. In the clinical context, it has been central to establish both a connectedness to Jung and a critical distance from him and from his writings and to increase an awareness of the diversity of the contemporary Jungian corpus. The term 'post-Jungian' that I introduced (in 1985) in my book 'Jung and the Post-Jungians'[1] serves as a useful heuristic indicator of what I have in

---

[1] Samuels, A. (1985) Jung and the Post-Jungians, London and Boston: Routledge and Kegan Paul.

mind. The term facilitates critical discussion of, for example, the clinical project of Michael Fordham and his colleagues in the Society of Analytical Psychology - or James Hillman's influential school of Archetypal Psychology.

It might be of interest briefly to recount my approach to the study of those themes that figured so prominently in the replies to my request for associations to 'Jung'. With regard to the relationship with Freud and its aftermath, I have tried to show (a) that there was a pre-Freudian or non-Freudian Jung (we can see this in his Zofingia Lectures of 1895 for example);[2] and (b) that there is a striking phenomenon to observe in which psychoanalysis takes up and renders consensual many ideas and practices that were controversial when first introduced or theorised by Jung. I do not do this in a spirit of showing Jung to have been a prophetic 'genius'. The intellectual framework has been a study of the way in which, within a profession, ideas and practices are sorted into hierarchies on the basis of affiliations and involving issues of power and leadership/discipleship. In other words, the proposition that psychoanalysis has taken on an increasingly 'Jungian' cast is presented in terms of the history of ideas rather than as a 'good result' for the Jungians. I consider competition, envy and the distortion of opposing views as motors of intellectual production within the field of depth psychology.[3]

As far as the allegations of anti-semitism and Nazism are concerned, I have made an extensive study of the whole issue, involving many publications that present new historical and archival material.[4] Succinctly, I believe that the critics of Jung are right to ask of contemporary analytical psychologists that they explore this particular part of the history of their profession. I conclude that, by doing this, analytical psychology can not only re-establish its ethical credentials but that there is much in what Jung was attempting, with disastrous results in his own personal case, in the psychological study of nationalism, national psychology and cul-

---

[2] See Jung, C. G. (1983) The Zofingia Lectures. Supplementary Volume A, Collected Works of C. G. Jung, London: Routledge.
[3] See Samuels, A, The Plural Psyche: Personality, Morality and the Father, , London and New York: Routledge,1989.
[4] I have expounded my arguments on this matter in Chapters 12 and 13 of The Political Psyche, London and New York: Routledge, 1993.

tural psychology that could form part of a contemporary approach to these issues. While there are important differences, I also think that the point made by philosophers and historians of philosophy concerning the need to continue to study Heidegger's texts (both in the context of his Nazi affiliation and, so to speak, relatively independently of that context) applies to analytical psychology and Jungian studies. In both instances, one task is to examine the degree to which involvement in the social events of the 1930s influenced the thinking of the two men.

As far as the notion that Jung was a 'mystic' or adhered to an 'occult' way (or even, as has recently been argued, that he started a 'cult') is concerned, I tend to approach this from the point of view of changing approaches to epistemology and support this with understandings gleaned from the history of science. Jung's approach to psychology challenged the observer-observed divide and foregrounded 'subjectivity' in the research process. I do not see him as the empiricist he claimed to be. Rather, I see him as fostering a systematic analysis or self-analysis by the observer of his or her responses to phenomena in the experienced world. I show in 'The Political Psyche' how contemporary clinical theorising about the analyst's countertransference greatly extends Jung's 'scientific' study of subjectivity leading to the possible usage of such an approach in relation to social and political thematics.[5]

Another problematizing response to 'Jung-as-mystic' has been to explore why the very idea excites such strong negative responses (save, perhaps, within departments of Religious Studies). We can see that the secular world has not completely evacuated religious responsiveness which we observe emerging in the West and beyond in the (widely differing) forms of religious fundamentalisms on the one hand and the 'New Age' phenomenon on the other. 'Spirituality' seems to be what many students want to study and I confess to not yet having evolved a complete answer to the problem of how to address this in a scholarly manner.[6]

---

[5] In Chapter 2.
[6] In their recent edited book Shadows of Spirit: Postmodernism and Religion (London and New York: Routledge, 1994), Philippa Berry and Andrew Wernick identify the same problem and their approach lends support to the strategy I have adopted.

Mapping Analytical Psychology in the University Context

I think the following areas of teaching and research exist.

1. Clinical research

Here I see three possibilities. The first concerns outcome studies and quantitative or qualitative approaches to issues of clinical efficacy. As a member of the Society for Psychotherapy Research and familiar with the literature, I do not see how most centres for psychoanalytic studies, as presently constituted and resourced, could undertake the large-scale controlled trials that are required. However, I can see an interesting angle in a comparative and critical study of the various protocols or statements of intent that psychotherapy researchers usually set out in their published proposals or reports. I have made a start in exploring from a meta-research angle some of the clinical assumptions that underpin the research projects themselves. The laying bare of these assumptions is of interest, not only in itself, but also in terms of the establishment of a series of outcome studies into the efficacy of long-term psychoanalytic/analytical psychotherapy. It is generally agreed that such studies are under-represented in the literature.

The second line of enquiry in clinical research concerns research into the clinical process. This would be mainly, though not exclusively, of interest to clinicians, and would focus, for example, on how practitioners employ the theoretical concepts with which they are equipped, or on how responses to particular kinds of material with which they are confronted by patients/clients are managed differently by different practitioners on the basis of theoretical orientation and personal variables (sex and ethnic background of practitioner and client, for example).

I have made a small start in researching how practitioners (approximately 30 in the sample) employ the various theoretical approaches to countertransference that exist.[7] As far as research

---

[7] Samuels, A, (1985b) 'Countertransference, the Mundus Imaginalis and a Research Project', Journal of Analytical Psychology, 30: 1.

approaches to countertransference that exist.[7] As far as research into the management of certain kinds of material is concerned, I carried out a survey involving nearly 700 analysts and psychotherapists (a cold-calling return rate of over 30%) from 14 different organisations of differing ideological orientation in 7 countries.[8]

A third possible avenue of research concerns (in general terms) overall practice issues such as the advisability and desirability of the practitioner explaining or describing to the client the likely nature, evolution and progress of the process he or she is undertaking. Classically, psychoanalysis has been reluctant to offer explanations of therapeutic principles and prognostications to the patient/client for many cogent reasons. However, when I proposed, in a letter to the 'British Journal of Psychiatry', that clinical practitioners might consider a controlled trial in which initial explanatory procedures were or were not employed, there was an interested response. A possible use of such research would also be in creating clear and reliable ways of informing the public generally (not just patients/clients) about the scope and experience of psychotherapeutic treatments.

It has been argued that research in 'difficult' areas such as psychoanalysis and psychotherapy is entering a new era. Following quantitative research and qualitative research, we are now in the stage of 'collaborative research'. This implies (but is not restricted to) involvement of patients/clients in the research at every point and at every level of it. I am interested in this argument and in seeing if and how feminist empirical research and oral historical research might inform such a project.

2. Research into assumptions underpinning clinical work

A contribution here would rest on studies of the ways in which psychoanalytic concepts and assumptions arise, not only in relation to shifting cultural norms and expectations, but also in (competitive) relation to other concepts and assumptions within

---

[7] Samuels, A, (1985b) 'Countertransference, the Mundus Imaginalis and a Research Project', Journal of Analytical Psychology, 30: 1.

[8] Samuels, A, (1993b) 'Replies to an International Questionnaire on Political Material brought into the Clinical Setting by Clients of Psychotherapists and Analysts'. International Review of Sociology, 100: 3.

psychoanalysis. For example, some Lacanian clinical practices, such as the variable length session, may be understood as a reaction, not only to cultural phenomena such as the valorisation of impulsiveness of 1950s and 1960s French Situationalism, but also as a negatively reactive response to the positive evaluation of regression in the clinical situation emerging from the British school of object relations. Here, the absolute reliability of the sessional frame, including its time boundaries, was being stressed by writers such as Balint and Winnicott.

The question one would ask of clinicians would concern the assumptions and concepts that they knew they rejected (and their reasons for this) as much as those they knew they had adopted.

As I hinted earlier, there is also a dimension in which the specificity of the individual practitioner needs to receive more attention. What is the role of the sex, sexual orientation, age, socioeconomic and ethnic background, and psychological type of practitioner in connection with the assumptions and concepts he or she utilises in clinical work?

3. *Teaching of the basic concepts of Jungian and post-Jungian analytical psychology.*

With regard to this key topic, I will make the general observation that many of Jung's central ideas underwent extensive revision in the course of his working life. However, because he was less concerned to systematise his thought than Freud, it is difficult to tease out the historical evolution of, for example, the theory of archetypes. 'The Collected Works of C. G. Jung' often presents important texts in a manner that makes a historical/variorum reading very difficult. Hence in the university, as opposed to the clinical context, the mutable and historical elements within Jung's theorising could be emphasised. I adopted this approach in 'A Critical Dictionary of Jungian Analysis' which has been useful in university-level teaching of analytical psychology here and abroad.[9]

---

[9] Samuels, A, Shorter, B and F Plaut, (1986) A Critical Dictionary of Jungian Analysis

4. Comparative Theoretical Studies

Teaching of analytical psychology should include comparisons with analogous theorising in all kinds of psychoanalysis (Kleinian, object relations, self-psychology, Lacanian and post-Lacanian, Laplanchian, etc.) as well as with humanistic and existential approaches. Moreover, there is a buried theory of group psychology in Jung's writings which can be recuperated and evaluated in comparison with psychoanalytic approaches to group processes.

5. Historical Approaches to Analytical Psychology.

In many centres for psychoanalytic studies, a great amount of the research undertaken is of a historical kind. This acts as a salutary inhibition on any claims psychoanalysis might make of a totalizing and universalistic nature. I have indicated my interest in Jung's activities in the 1930s but there are some other areas that I would like to continue to explore. Recently, I published a history of the professionalization of analytical psychology (mainly in Britain) entitled 'The Professionalization of Carl G. Jung's Analytical Psychology Clubs' and I would like to extend this interest so as to relate the history of psychoanalysis as a profession to other historical researches into the emergence of contemporary professions from about 1840 onwards.

I am presently working on two small historical projects. The first concerns the establishment, flourishing and eventual demise of the Medical Section of the British Psychological Society from 1937 to 1975 as a forum where psychoanalysts and analytical psychologists might meet on friendly and equal terms to exchange ideas. I have obtained the co-operation of the British Psychological Society and have unearthed a good deal of interesting material including minute books, correspondence and so forth. Many of the great names of immediate pre-war and post-war psychoanalysis were part of this Section (Winnicott, Bion, Segal, Sutherland, Rickman etc.) as well as leading Jungians such as Fordham, Adler, Plaut, Prince and Lambert. I hope to be able to offer some ideas about the set of historical and cultural circumstances that made such a collaboration possible, and those which brought it to an end. I am in the process of establishing what relevant materials might exist in the archives of the Society of Analytical Psychology and the British Psycho-Analytical Society.

My second 'live' historical project concerns the controversial correspondence between C. G. Jung and his assistant C. A. Meier (based in Zürich) and Professor Matthias Göring and his colleagues at the German Institute of Psychotherapy in Berlin between 1933 and 1940. I have managed to obtain extensive archival materials from the C. G. Jung and C. A. Meier archives in Zürich and from the archives of the German Society for Analytical Psychology.

6. Applications of analytical psychology in other fields.

Important interests for me are explorations of possible intersections of analytical psychology with social and political theory and the general applicability of a psychoanalytic contribution to the study of political institutions and processes. I would hope to contribute, for example, to a multi-disciplinary critique of existing models of leadership and citizenship and also to an exploration of whether or not we may justifiably speak in terms of a psychology of social connectedness as well as of a psychology founded on notions of lack, rupture and castration. I would like to contribute my work on social aspects of Jung's concept of the 'psychoid unconscious' to this ongoing discussion in which I imagine a good deal of reflexive, mutually critical examination would take place. Psychoanalytic theory is located within many of the phenomena it attempts to survey, something the profession has tended to overlook.

Then there is also a contribution that can be made by analytical psychology to literary criticism and the history of art. Here, much will depend on the specific interests of different research students. My own interest has been with the exploration of imagistic themes in an intertextual manner. For example, I have studied the twin images of 'nature' and 'trickster' in a comparative study of works by Margaret Atwood and J-K Huysmans.[10]

Contemporary images of tricksters, especially female images, are of interest to me at the moment. I have been studying the female private investigator genre, the emergence of the figure of the 'crone' in the works of some feminist fiction and non-fiction writers, and the impact on general cultural sensibility of texts that

---

[10] In chapter 5 of The Political Psyche.

feature the consensual lesbian sado-masochist as protagonist. These may be taken as illustrative of contemporary images of female tricksters.

Analytical psychology can make a contribution to gender studies, cultural studies and lesbian and gay studies. Whilst the classical theory of animus and anima is often contested nowadays, there is increasing academic interest in how to explore images of men and women held by men and women, taking these as indicators of contemporary fears and fantasies. In post-Jungian analytical psychology, there is a good deal of work on theories of gender construction and of sexual difference, whilst Jung's rejection of the idea that homosexual sexual orientation is perverse or in itself pathological provides a useful basis for a contribution to the study of dissident sexualities.[11]

Many Jungian analysts have hoped to deploy analytical psychology in a psychological account of the social phenomena of ethnicity and 'race'. I have to admit to some doubts about this. Instead, I would reframe the issue in terms of a consideration of the role of universalizing discourses within both analytical psychology and psychoanalysis in preventing the formation of transcultural approaches to psychology and psychotherapy.

Traditionally, analytical psychology has been of interest to academics working in the field of religious studies. My experience in several universities has been that this is where one might well find careful and critical readings of Jungian texts taking place.

Other possibilities for collaborative, multi-disciplinary work on applications of analytical psychology may exist in philosophy, law, anthropology and psychology. As far as psychology is concerned, my experience has been that there is still interest in Jung's role as the originator of the Word Association Test and of the theory of psychological types, as well as his influence on Henry Murray in

---

[11] My own work on masculinity and the father, in and since the edited volume, The Father: Contemporary Jungian Perspectives. London: Free Association Books; New York: New York University Press, 1985, may be cited here.

the evolution of the Thematic Apperception Tests and on projective testing generally.

Teaching and Psychoanalysis: A Necessary Impossibility

Paul Verhaeghe

'The strange behaviour of patients, in being able to combine a conscious knowing with not knowing, remains inexplicable by what is called normal psychology.'[1]

However different the Freud biographies may be, they are unanimous on one point: Freud wanted to know. From the outset, we see an ambitious man at work whose goal is to reach a Master position through knowledge. When he takes his first steps towards psychoanalysis - he is at that stage middle-aged - his goal is still the same, and this colours both his initial theory and practice. The analytic cure is a search for lost knowledge, lost as a result of it becoming unconscious; the aim of the treatment is the re-inscription of this unconscious knowledge into Consciousness. The implicit expectation is that the therapeutic effects will follow automatically. In this respect, Freud reveals himself as an inheritor of the Enlightenment, in his belief that the mere transmission of knowledge is enough to induce change. Nevertheless, beyond this Enlightenment, we meet Socrates with his insistent questions: what is knowledge, and how can it be passed on or taught? These are the two questions I want to address in this paper.

With respect to the first question, I have to specify that the knowledge concerned is rather particular: it is the knowledge that is searched for by every subject right from the start. The Dora case study illustrates the insistency and gives us the gist of this search: through her symptoms and dreams, Dora continually asks what it means to be a woman and a daughter in relation to the desire of a man.[2]

---

[1] S. Freud, S.E. XII, p.142
[2] S. Freud, Fragment of an Analysis of a Case of Hysteria (1905e), S.E.VII.

Teaching Transference

This particular illustration receives a general characterization when Freud begins to study childhood and thus discovers the generality of what he calls the infantile sexual researches, i.e. the original quest for knowledge. Just like the hysterical patient, the child wants to know the answer to three related questions. The first concerns the difference between boys and girls; the second question concerns the origin of babies; the last question is about the father and the mother: what is their relationship? The child, says Freud, proceeds like a scientist and will forge genuinely explanatory theories, that is why Freud calls them infantile sexual researches and infantile sexual theories.³ The recurring problem with the knowledge produced is that the answers are never definitive, with the result that the questions persist. This was also the case with Dora, whose second dream mentions that 'Sie fragt wohl hundertmal', she asks a hundred times.⁴ According to Freud, the infantile sexual researches falter on two specific points: the role of the father ('the fertilising role of the semen') and the female sexual identity ('the existence of the female sexual orifice'), and this failure, says Freud, ends 'in a renunciation which not infrequently leaves behind it a permanent injury of the instinct for knowledge'.⁵ Instead of a correct knowledge, the child must content itself with the primary fantasies, combining true, false and lack of knowledge into imaginary constructions. This, of course, will strengthen Freud's conviction that neurosis is either the effect of an incorrect knowledge in these matters, or the effect of a lack of knowledge.

Consequently, the first therapeutic solution proposed by Freud consists of providing patients with what he considers to be the right knowledge, thus putting the therapist in the position of the Master. A perfect illustration can be found in the construction produced for the benefit of little Hans: 'Long before he (i.e. Hans) was in the world, I had known that a little Hans would come who would be so fond of his mother that he would be bound to feel afraid of his father because of it …' Hans's reaction is very revealing: 'Does the Professor talk to God, Hans asked his father on the way home, as he can tell all that beforehand?' This little interaction is very instructive: it shows the analyst in the position of possessing,

---

3. S. Freud, Three Essays on the Theory of Sexuality (1905d), S.E. VII, pp. 194-197.
4. S. Freud, (1905e), S.E. VII, p. 97.
5. S. Freud, S.E. VII, *o.c.*, p. 197.

Teaching and Psychoanalysis

teaching and guaranteeing the correctness of a knowledge.[6] Again, the Dora case study demonstrates extensive clinical applicability. Freud assumes the role of the Master who knows in matters of desire and jouissance, and who, by way of treatment, teaches this knowledge to the patient; the patient must accept these insights; and so on. And again, the generalization of this conception can be found in his ideas on sexual enlightenment. In 1907 he writes enthusiastically on the subject: the adult may not withhold the necessary knowledge, on the contrary, he has to inform children correctly, in order that their incorrect, fantasmatic birth theories may become superfluous.[7] For Freud, it is obvious that a general enlightenment will result in a drastic drop in the numbers of neurotic adults.

This generalization has a very strong impact on the treatment: the cure is transformed into didactics, the didactics become a cure. A perfect illustration of this confusion can be found in the famous Introductory Lectures on Psychoanalysis, the Vorlesungen - that is, literally, 'What is read in front of the pupils'. Both the treatment and the didactics amount to what I want to consider as a 'didactical analysis of resistance'. At that time, Freud became a real Master in discerning the resistances and antagonisms of his pupils/patients, even before they knew them themselves. Time and again, he formulates the critique of his pupils/patients himself - much better than they ever could have done themselves - and each time he takes the edge off the argument.

Such a strategy can only result in two possible reactions: either one is transformed from a patient into a pupil who says yes and absorbs everything, or one reacts as Dora did, by slamming the door and leaving. From a historical point of view, this will give birth to the analysis of the resistance, i.e. the struggle to convince the patient. If she or he does not want to accept the presented knowledge, that is a matter of resistance. No wonder that Freud

---

[6.] Note the 'Professor' form of address! S. Freud, *Analysis of a Phobia in a Five-Year-Old Boy* (1909b), S.E. X, p. 42.
[7.] S. Freud, *The Sexual Enlightenment of Children* (1907c). S.E. IX, p. 131.

Teaching Transference

considers educatability to be the determining factor of fitness for psychoanalytic treatment.[8]

From a psychoanalytic point of view, both reactions represent a failure: the group that remains is transformed into obedient followers who take in knowledge; the individuals who leave remain unknowing; both of them are identical in that sense that neither of them surpasses the knowledge of the Other. It does not take Freud long to recognise this common point of failure. Indeed, whether the patient gives a categorical 'yes' or 'no' to an interpretation, both answers are suspect and amount to the same thing: the patient has not accepted the interpretation. Both of them are an effect of something different, something that will become more and more important: the transference relationship by which the analyst is ascribed or refused the position of the master.

Based on this experience, Freud will change his course drastically: knowledge must not be provided by the analyst, on the contrary it is the analysand who has to produce knowledge, and the position of the teaching Master becomes forbidden for the analyst during the course of the treatment.[9] Instead of teaching, the analyst has to be taught. Instead of the analyst's signifiers, those of the patient fill the scene; the patient is the one who knows, only he doesn't know himself that he knows. Knowledge coming from an external source is merely an inhibiting factor. This is clearly expressed in Freud's technical advice from this period: ideally the patient should not read analytic works, the analyst should restrain from giving precocious information and interpretation, etc.[10] The distance separating the Dora case study from the Rat Man analysis is tremendous in this respect. In the latter case study, he confirms explicitly the futility of explicative interventions.[11] In matters of clinical practice, all attention goes to the creation of a situation in, and by which, the patient can produce as many signifiers as possible.

---

[8]. 'The qualification which is the determining factor of fitness for psycho-analytic treatment - *that is, whether the patient is educable ...*', S. Freud, *On Psychotherapy* (1905a), S.E. VII, p. 264, my italics.

[9]. This change is expressed at its best in Freud's comment on the Irma dream, cf. The Interpretation of Dreams, S.E. IV, p. 108.

[10]. S. Freud, On Beginning the Treatment (1913c), S.E. XII, pp. 139-142.

[11]. S. Freud, Notes upon a Case of Obsessional Neurosis (1909d), S.E. X, p. 181 n. 1 and p. 185, n. 2.

Teaching and Psychoanalysis

From a Lacanian point of view, this can be described as the operational character of the transference, i.e. the transference as driving force of the treatment. The analysand expects knowledge from the analyst; actually, at the beginning of the treatment, the analyst doesn't know anything at all about this particular patient, but he can use his position in such a way that it makes the patient produce signifiers, i.e. knowledge, for the one-who-is-supposed-to-know. That is one of the reasons why Freud stated that an analysis can only start where the transference is 'positive', and thus entails an abundant associative production. A negative transference, on the other hand, results in silence and must be dispensed with as soon as possible.

This change in direction - knowledge located in the analysand, not in the analyst - is not a final one. A new stumbling block arises with this reversal. Freud experienced this in the epistemological domain when he studied the infantile sexual theories, which taught him the difference between knowledge and something beyond knowledge, something that belongs to another register, a register other than the Symbolic Order. It is at this point that the enlightenment - indeed, the Enlightenment - falls short.[12] The same goes for the treatment: there is something that cannot be put into words, something for which words are lacking; originally he considered this to be the traumatic experience, but later on he calls it the 'mycelium', the 'nucleus of our being', the 'originally repressed'.

Freud faces a second difficulty here that will take on more and more the shape of an impossibility. In the first half of his analytic career, he was more or less convinced of the fact that the 'last word', the ultimate knowledge, could be found, provided the treatment went far enough; in a later stage, he has to conclude that verbalization is only possible up to a certain point; beyond that, there lies another order, the order of the Beyond the Pleasure Principle, meaning beyond the representations (Vorstellungen, i.e. signifiers). Knowledge as it appears in the signifier is not final, there is a beyond. With Lacan, we meet here the dimension of the

---

[12.] In 1933, he concludes that he has grossly overrated the prophylactic effect of enlightenment: although it installs a conscious knowledge, it does not stop the children from building up their fantasies. Knowledge is not enough, there is another factor at work. S. Freud, Analysis Terminable and Interminable (1937c). S.E. XXIII, pp. 233-234.

truth, and in particular a typical feature of the truth: it can only be half said, 'le mi-dire de la vérité'.

Why do we call it 'truth', how does it differ from mere knowledge? One could answer that truth always concerns desire and jouissance, but the same goes for the Freudian knowledge from the very beginning, e.g. his ideas about Lust (pleasure) and Wunsch (wish). The essential characteristic of truth is that it confronts us with the ultimate point where knowledge about desire and jouissance can no longer be put into words. Knowledge itself always stays within the realm of the signifier, truth starts within this realm but evokes a dimension beyond it, that is the main reason why we invented poetry. This ultimate dimension of desire and jouissance is the driving part of it - and driving comes from drive. This dimension beyond the signifier is the Lacanian Real, or, to be more specific, the lost 'object a' that is forever lacking for the speaking subject, causing his ever shifting desire.

With this, Freud stumbles upon a second impossibility. The one discussed above concerned the fact that it is impossible for the analyst to assume the knowledge-producing and knowledge-guaranteeing Master position. The second one concerns something that applies to every speaking subject, namely, the impossibility of saying everything and of producing the final knowledge.

The first one finds its best formulation in 1933, when he enumerates the three impossible professions: mastering, educating, analysing.[13] It is impossible for any person to impersonate the truth ('and only the truth, nothing but the truth') for another person, which is precisely what is required by those three professions. Freud knew very well what he was talking about, as he himself had even tried to combine them: in his early period, therapy came down to teaching from a Master position.

The second impossibility will be elaborated in Beyond the Pleasure Principle; the elaboration itself faces a fundamental difficulty, as it concerns something that lies beyond the dimension of the signifier, and thus beyond normal knowledge. Something keeps on insisting beyond the representations, the repetition compulsion is a desperate attempt to bind it with signifiers in order

---

[13] In the paragraph preceding this threefold impossibility, he states that analysis and the analytic relationship is based 'on the love of truth - that is, on a recognition of reality'. S. Freud, 'Analysis Terminable and Interminable' (1937c), S.E. XXIII, p. 248.

Teaching and Psychoanalysis

to Master it, but this fails time and again. This something has to do with the drive, albeit with that part of the drive that lies beyond the pleasure principle and that aims at another finality. Freud's first elaborations are situated both in the field of the traumatic neuroses (the present post-traumatic stress disorders) and in children's games, thus illustrating the general character of this 'beyond'.

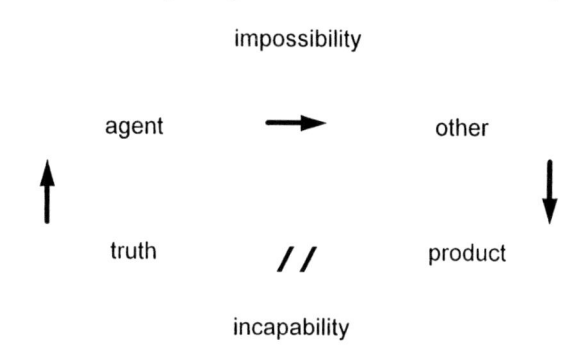

$$
\begin{array}{ccc}
& \text{impossibility} & \\
\text{agent} & \longrightarrow & \text{other} \\
\uparrow & & \downarrow \\
\text{truth} & // & \text{product} \\
& \text{incapability} &
\end{array}
$$

What does not become clear with Freud, is the link between these two impossibilities. They are linked in the sense that each of them tries to answer the other: assuming the Master position functions as a guarantee for the answer that covers the lack in the chain of signifiers, and, vice versa, the cover of the lack in the Symbolic corroborates the position of the master: 'the father who knew long before the subject was born ...' Lacan's theory of the four discourses makes it possible to chart those two impossibilities with their respective interdependence; moreover, this theory demonstrates the structurally determined interactions between them, through the four different discourses.[14] Each discourse

---

[14.] As we consider this theory to be a condensation of Lacan's evolution, any bibliographic reference to a particular part of his work is too limited. The theory itself was coined during the seminar of 1969-70, L'Envers de la psychanalyse (Paris, Seuil, 1991, pp. 1-246), Radiophonie (Scilicet, 1970, nr.2/3, pp. 55 - 99) and the next seminar: D'un discours qui ne serait pas du semblant. A further elaboration can be found in Encore, the seminar of 1972-73 (Paris, Seuil, 1975, pp. 1-135).
For a didactic exposition, I refer the English reader to: P.Verhaeghe, 'From impossibility to inability: Lacan's theory on the four discourses', in The Letter, Lacanian perspectives on

consists of the same formal structure: it starts with an agent driven by a truth to speak to another with as a result a product; nevertheless, it is impossible for the agent to transmit his message completely to this other; this impossibility is founded on an underlying incapability: each discourse is incapable of producing something that would embrace its very starting-point, i.e. the truth. Both the impossibility and incapability are the effect of the radical heteronomy of the truth: part of it lies beyond the signifier and belongs to the realm of the jouissance.

The four positions of this formal structure can be occupied by four different terms, by which the particularity of each concrete discourse is determined.[15] This theory enables Lacan to formalise the three impossible Freudian professions as three different discourses, each of them with a particular appearance of the impossibility. The impossible regieren is the discourse of the master; the impossible edukieren the university discourse; the impossible analysieren the analytic discourse. He even adds a fourth one: the impossible desire installs the discourse of the hysteric. These four discourses are closely related in the sense that there is a structurally determined shift from one to the other, as the impossibility of one discourse results in/is answered by the impossibility of the next discourse.[16]

The particular advantage of this theory for our subject - knowledge and its transmission through psychoanalysis versus the transmission of psychoanalytic knowledge - is that it focuses on the transference with respect to the relationship between knowledge (a term) and truth (a position), and this in a purely formal manner, that is, independent from any particular content of any particular patient. Indeed, every discourse represents a social bond that elicits

---

Psychoanalysis, 4, Spring 1995, Dublin, pp. 76-100; and P Verhaeghe, Does woman exist? From Freud's Hysteric to Lacan's Feminine, Rebus Press Ltd., London, 1996.
[15]. The four elements are:
the S_1, standing for the master; it is the signifier with which a subject pretends to be complete, without any division at all;
the S_2, denominating the endless chain of signifiers and thus standing for knowledge;
'object a' is what lies beyond the signifier, the primordial object that is irrevocably lost due to the acquisition of language;
$\mathcal{S}$ is the divided and barred subject, barred from the Real and divided between the signifiers.
[16]. See Addendum.

another social bond by its failure, that is, another discourse with another relationship to knowledge and truth. The application of this discourse theory will permit us to chart the relationship between teaching and analysis as a necessary one between two impossibilities.

The relationship between analyst and patient forms the kernel of the analytic practice and determines this practice in a twofold way. First of all, the relationship must be made productive so that the patient produces signifiers; secondly, the relationship itself must be worked on. The first aspect induces knowledge, the second concerns truth.

The productivity of the transference relationship consists in the fact that the patient ascribes to the analyst the position of the-one-who-knows, and that is why the patient produces signifiers, for this Other-who-is-supposed-to-know. At this stage, analysis can be understood in terms of a 'Master discourse'. Indeed, from the point of view of the patient, the analyst is situated at the place of the agent as a Master S_1, and that is why the patient at the place of the other produces signifiers S_2, and so, produces knowledge:

$$S_1 \longrightarrow S_2$$

This first stage during an analysis results in a considerable growth in knowledge. That is why Lacan considered psychoanalysis an effective remedy against ignorance. An appropriate name for this first stage could be a Socratic discourse: the analyst functions as the proverbial midwife, enabling the patient to formulate a knowledge already there.

Inevitably, that is, structurally, the next step in this discourse is the production of 'object small a', beyond the knowledge that can be expressed in signifiers:

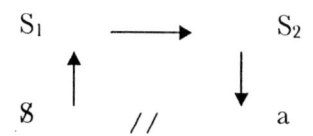

$$\begin{array}{ccc} S_1 & \longrightarrow & S_2 \\ \uparrow & & \downarrow \\ \$ & // & a \end{array}$$

Teaching Transference

This second stage implies the limit of the Master discourse, which means that we are faced with two possibilities: either there is a regression, or a progression from it to another discourse.

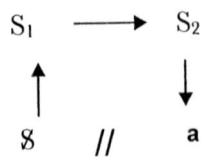

$$S_1 \longrightarrow S_2$$
$$\uparrow \qquad \downarrow$$
$$\$ \quad // \quad a$$

The regression brings us to the 'University discourse', where knowledge as such is staged as the agent.

$$S_2 \longrightarrow a \longrightarrow \$$$

This regression was the Freudian choice for a very long time, where Freud hoped that knowledge as such would be sufficient to bridge the gap between a subject and its object of desire. The result is exactly the opposite of expected, because the product of this discourse is an ever increasing division of the subject:

In this light, it is perfectly understandable that Freud's last paper, Die Ichspaltung im Abwehrvorgang, goes about a generalised splitting of the subject.[17] The conclusion is quite clear: producing an ever increasing mass of knowledge, i.e. signifiers, intensifies the loss of 'object a' for the pupil and leaves him all the more divided. To put it bluntly: the more you know, the more you will hesitate.

The path of progression, on the other hand, brings us to the paradoxes of the 'Analytic discourse'. There we find knowledge, i.e. the body of signifiers, at the position of the truth. Lacan expresses it as follows: 'What one expects from an analyst is that he makes his

---

[17] S. Freud, Splitting of the Ego in the Process of Defence (1940c). S.E. XXIII.

knowledge function in terms of truth'. This is impossible, and thus he continues: 'That is why he restricts himself to half-speaking'.[18]

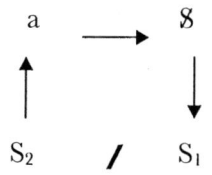

$$\begin{array}{ccc} a & \longrightarrow & \$ \\ \uparrow & & \downarrow \\ S_2 & / & S_1 \end{array}$$

This S_2 is the body of signifiers, produced by the patient in analysis, during its logically first stage.[19] Indeed, the beginning of treatment does not consist in an analytic discourse, but makes it possible, because it obliges the patient to produce this ever increasing body of knowledge. With the analytic discourse, this body of signifiers gives rise to what lies beyond it, 'object a', and turns it into the agent of this discourse, which causes the division of the subject and his desire. As a product of this discourse, the subject will be confronted with an S_1 of his own.

The difference between these two possibilities, regression and progression, is considerable. In the regressive solution, the analyst acts as the incarnation of knowledge, in the progressive one, he is nothing but a support of object a. The first solution is an attempt to keep the Master discourse going at a lower level, the second one is radically different, in the sense that the relationship as such, between the one-supposed-to-know and the-one-producing-knowledge, ends in an exact reversal. Indeed, the Analytic discourse is a reversed Master discourse. The choice for a psychoanalytic solution requires this reversal of positions, that is, the working through of the transference relationship at the point where the analyst was installed in the position of guarantor of the truth. The net and always unpredictable result of this working through resides in the way a subject is able to tolerate the existence of the fundamental lack in the Symbolic, without a need either to fill it up, to disavow it or to reject it.

---

[18] 'Half-speaking' is an attempt to translate 'mi-dire', a neologism in French. J.Lacan, Le Séminaire livre XVII: L'envers de la psychanalyse, Paris, Seuil, 1991, p.58. A further elaboration can be found in: Le Séminaire, livre XX: Encore, Paris, Seuil, ch. 8.
[19] Indeed, logically; as a 'stage', it never stops.

Teaching Transference

This theory of the four discourses enables me to discuss now the relationship between analysis and teaching in a structural way, by focusing on the elements of transference, knowledge and truth. The crucial difference lies in the different goals, which I would like to delineate as follows: separation for psychoanalysis, alienation for teaching. In terms of discourse, these goals imply that teaching aims at the transmission of knowledge, while analysis focuses on the co-optation of truth as the cause operating beyond knowledge.

First, teaching. Education always amounts to the process of passing signifiers, and thus knowledge, from the teacher to the pupil; this passing is only effective on condition that there is a positive transference: one learns where one loves. This can be understood perfectly in Freudian terms: with a primitive organism, the incorporation of the external world is limited to the pleasurable part of it, the rest is expulsed/repressed (cf. 'I could not take it in'); with the acquisition of language, incorporation takes place by way of signifiers and becomes an identification: the subject identifies itself with the signifiers of the Other, i.e. the knowledge offered by this Other, still on condition of a positive transference with this Other. From a Lacanian point of view, this identification is always an alienation: taking in signifiers coming from the Other turns the subject ontologically into a stranger for itself (Cf. Rimbaud: 'Je est un autre', 'I is another'). This alienation implies both gain and loss. First of all, there is a gain in knowledge, but the process goes much further than that, because the alienation is the very operation by which the relationship between subject and Other is established. Depending on the number of signifiers taken in by the subject, the corresponding external reality grows; even more so: this reality is thus realised because it is precisely determined by the Symbolic Order.[20] On the other hand, we have a loss, which is structurally determined and concerns firstly the Real, more particularly the loss-of-being, 'le manque-à-être', and secondly the Symbolic, more particularly the loss of choice: one's own desire is always alienated to the desire of the Other.

---

[20]. The inspiration for this part of Lacanian theory lies definitely with M. Klein, especially her paper on: 'The Importance of Symbol-Formation in the Development of the Ego', I.J.Psa., 1930, 11. See Lacan, Freud's papers on technique: Seminar I, ch. 6-7, and *The four fundamental concepts on psycho-analysis: Seminar XI*, ch. 16-19.

These effects apply to the pupils for whom teaching always results in an effect of unification (group formation) in which each particular subject is drawn and drowned. For the teacher the act of teaching - producing signifiers - results inevitably in a confrontation with the limits of this knowledge, and thus with that part of the truth that lies beyond verbalization. This is the structural reason why teaching can be considered an impossible profession.

Next, analysis. Here, the process moves in the opposite direction, albeit also under transference: it is the analysand who produces signifiers and thus knowledge for the analyst who is on the receiving end. This time, he is the one who has to be taught, with the result that the alienation is situated on his side, entailing the risk that he identifies himself with the knowledge that is produced for him and ascribed to him. In contrast, on part of the analysand, the possibility of bypassing the alienation is created. Indeed, in so far as the subject keeps on producing signifiers for the analyst in the position of the one who knows, the subject is accordingly confronted with the alienating character of these signifiers with respect to 'his' identity as a subject: 'For in this labour which he undertakes to reconstruct for another, he rediscovers the fundamental alienation that made him construct it like another, and which has always destined it to be taken from him by another'.[21] In this sense, the analytic work is closely related to the work of mourning, and results in a desalienation or desidentification. This work confronts the subject with the irreparable lack that lies at the heart of the Symbolic. This is the same lack where the infantile search for knowledge came to a standstill for the same reasons: the symbolic sexual identity, the function of the father, the sexual rapport. The Symbolic can never embrace these aspects of the Real; as a lack, it opens the void for the subject, leaving him with two possibilities.[22] In the first place, the analysand may recoil at this confrontation with the lack, and returns to the answer produced and guaranteed by the master; hence, he remains within the alienation and stays subjected to the

---

[21] J.Lacan, Function and field of speech and language, in: Ecrits, a selection, W.W.Norton, New York, 1977, p.42.
[22] In our opinion, Bion conceptualises the same inconceivable thing with his ideas on 'O'; cf. *Attention and Interpretation*, London, Karnac Books Ltd., 1984.

desire of the Other and his knowledge: he remains a pupil. Consequently, he enters the group and shares the group's knowledge; to couch it in the linguistic terminology of F. de Saussure: he shares the conventions of the signifiers used by that group to cover the Real. In the second, the analysand can engage in a confrontation with the truth, that is, with the fundamental lack in the Other; hence, he will reduce the answer of the Master to an answer, by which the possibility of separation is opened. Beyond the dimension of knowledge, the subject has co-opted the truth: there is no guaranteeing Other. Consequently, the next step can only be indicated, but cannot be filled in. From this point onwards, the subject can come to the act of creativity, albeit a creatio ex nihilo, obliging him to make choices of his own. The determinism of the alienation is replaced by the semi-determinism of the separation; the time in which this takes place is the future anterior, the 'I shall have been for what I am in the process of becoming'; choices made now determine the future.[23] Compared to the process of teaching, which resulted in the homogenization of the pupils into a group (and left the teacher divided), analysis ends with the production of the radical difference between the analysands (and risks leaving the analyst in alienation).[24] It is no coincidence that Lacan discusses the creatio ex nihilo in his seminar on ethics: the choices one has to make beyond this point are arbitrary ones (there is no guarantee), and thus ethical ones.

Due to its structure, separation cannot be taught, but teaching is the necessary precondition for it: a sufficient amount of supporting signifiers has to be produced, before one can reach the point of lack of support. Once that point is reached, every signifier fails. I am reminded of an expression of my friend and colleague B. Driessens: 'trying to catch the truth with words is just like trying to catch water with a net: the only thing caught is dirt'.

---

[23] J.Lacan, 'Function and field of speech and language', in: *Ecrits*, a selection, W.W.Norton, New York, 1977, p. 86. See also: *The Seminar, book I, Freud's papers on technique*, Cambridge University Press, 1988, p. 158.

[24] This is expressed in the final paragraph of Lacan's XIth seminar, *The four fundamental concepts of psycho-analysis*.

Teaching and Psychoanalysis

Historically speaking, it is only the jester who is permitted, not to formulate but to evoke the truth; in this sense the analyst is the actual incarnation of the buffoon.

The difference between providing someone with signifiers and making someone produce signifiers, i.e. the difference between teaching as a Master or being taught as a supposed Master, can be used to make a differentiation between psychotherapy and psychoanalysis. Within the realm of the so-called supporting therapy, the treatment comes down to the fact that the therapist takes the position of the guaranteeing Other and provides the patient with the correct signifiers. Historically speaking, that is even where psychotherapy started, with the Greek theatre that demonstrated for the public their own drama, thus permitting them to identify with the players and resulting in what Aristotle called the catharsis. This kind of therapy permits the subject to elaborate a symbolic framework with which to tackle the Real. Psychoanalysis is a possible sequel, in which the subject has acquired enough signifiers in order to question the alienation and to come to the separation.

To conclude: transference can be used in a twofold way, either to pass signifiers on or to make someone produce them. In both cases, producing signifiers, whether in the position of teacher or of analysand, confronts the subject inevitably with the point of lack, and opens the possibility of an analytic process. In the first case, teaching is the main goal, it gives rise to alienation and transmission of knowledge, resulting in group formation around shared signifiers, i.e. doxa. For the Master, however, it provokes a confrontation with the lack in the Symbolic order and obliges him to question his own position as a divided subject towards this lack. In the second case, analysis becomes the aim, it gives rise to separation and co-optation of the truth, confronting the analysand with his own subjectivity, his other-ness. For the analyst, however, it opens the trap of an identification with the Master position, from which he must stay away. The two processes are narrowly related. The discourse of the Master instils knowledge, but produces the 'object a' in such a way that it cannot be related to the divided subject. The analytic discourse starts beyond this knowledge, with this 'object a' in the position of the agent in a causal relationship to the divided subject, who produces an S_1 of his own.

Teaching Transference

The internal antinomy between those two processes finds its clearest expression in what are called the psychoanalytic 'schools' and their ever-present difficulty: how is it possible to form a group with people who have reached the pinnacle of their other-ness?

Teaching and Psychoanalysis

Addendum

The four terms: S_1 and S_2, $barred{S}$ and a, stand in a fixed order. With respect to the fixed order, they can be rotated over the positions, with as a result four different forms of discourse. Indeed, with the fifth rotation, one returns to the starting point, due to the fixed order of the term.

The discourse of the Master:

$$\uparrow \frac{S_1}{\barred{S}} \longrightarrow \frac{S_2}{a} \downarrow \; //$$

shifts to the University discourse:

$$\uparrow \frac{S_2}{S_1} \longrightarrow \frac{a}{\barred{S}} \downarrow \; //$$

shifts to the Analytic discourse:

$$\uparrow \frac{a}{S_2} \longrightarrow \frac{\barred{S}}{S_1} \downarrow \; //$$

which in its turn gives rise to the Hysteric's discourse:

$$\uparrow \frac{\barred{S}}{a} \longrightarrow \frac{S_1}{S_2} \downarrow \; //$$

43

Thinking Psychoanalytically in the University
Karl Figlio

The future of psychoanalytic studies is tied to the university. The university is the only institution dedicated to testing one form of knowledge against another, and of promoting a discipline in the interest of knowledge itself. The difference between psychoanalysis and psychoanalytic studies resides mainly in the fact that psychoanalysis requires working with the unconscious in the transference, while psychoanalytic studies requires working with other disciplines. To pursue the former, one normally works with an analyst, a supervisor and a patient; to pursue the latter, one follows an interest in psychoanalysis as both an object of inquiry and a way of throwing light on other fields. Psychoanalytic studies, therefore, is a university subject.

On the face of it, psychoanalytic studies also has a different aim from teaching psychoanalysis, and should be kept separate from the trend towards bringing psychoanalytic training into universities. The case for university-based psychoanalytic training is generally that it provides a secure, reputable institutional base, a rigorous theoretical grounding and a way out of sectarian allegiances. Psychoanalytic studies, on the other hand, does not aim to train clinicians, and is free to think of psychoanalysis as a form of knowledge and to make use of it wherever it seems helpful. Just as a river cuts a channel partly by complying with the terrain around it, psychoanalytic studies will carve a path into established university disciplines, while they also resist and redirect it. It will take shape and change shape, like any other field.

In earlier papers, I argued that theory could be separated from clinical practice and developed in its own right.[1] Not that psychoanalytic knowledge was to be hived off from the clinic - far from it - but that it could be freed from an inhibiting worry about training and about regulating practice. The ethical and professional con-

---

[1] Figlio, K (1993), 'The future of analytical psychotherapy: what do we profess?', Free Associations no. 29 4(1): 87-98;and (1993), 'The field of psychotherapy: conceptual and ethical definitions', British Journal of Psychotherapy 9(3): 324-35.

cerns that impede free inquiry could be handled under law dealing with practices and services more generally. Reassured by this legal umbrella, one could attend to the idea of a field based on research, rather than factions based on identification. I chose one example - primary narcissism - to show the importance to the field of psychoanalysis of a theoretical core that maps the terrain of inquiry and informs the generation of new knowledge.

I would like to develop this notion of a field, and focus on a defining feature of psychoanalytic studies. In my view, the diverse streams of psychoanalytic studies need to have more in common than, separately, each has with another field. The core notion, which could hold the field together, is 'thinking psychoanalytically'; and even though psychoanalytic studies is not a clinical discipline, thinking psychoanalytically nonetheless involves a form of transference.

Recent events have opened opportunities for developing the field in Britain. Several universities now offer degree schemes in psychoanalytic studies. A few have either established trainings in psychoanalytic psychotherapy or are considering affiliation with training organisations. The Universities Association for Psychoanalytic Studies and the Universities Psychotherapy Association have a substantial university membership. There is, therefore, also an institutional location for the field.

Three features of this new university subject stand out. First, universities have followed the lead of Kent, and are establishing centres and departments of psychoanalytic studies. Second, pressure upon universities to diversify and take part in practical training has coincided with an insecurity among private training organisations, to produce an interest in university-based clinical programmes. Third, there has been a proliferation of theoretical orientations.

In the past, with principally a Lacanian orientation and no clinical input, psychoanalytic studies was part of cultural studies, broadly speaking. It developed from a close relationship between a limited range of theory and an object of study (as in Lacanian film study), and could be codified and made useable in these other fields. Now, however, programmes and publications encompass a variety of orientations in the broadly-defined British 'Object Relations School' and analytical psychology as well. With the institutional base, the diversity of psychoanalytic theory and a training/clinical dimension, it is pulling away from, say, cultural studies, and is drawing itself into a field in its own right.

If one studies the growth of scientific thinking in the 17th - 19th centuries, one sees a differentiation of empirical and experimental domains from a web of knowledges.[2] In the logical positivist tradition, which is equivalent to modern scientific ideology, this separating out of a scientific domain constituted a freeing up of inquiry from bonds of ideology, dogma and metaphysics. It is a narrow view of the development of a field, from which the history and philosophy of science have retrieved an understanding of science as a cultural activity.

In psychoanalytic studies, there are continuous emergings, submergings and re-emergings, as the field falls into other subjects and reappears; and there is a self-conscious concern with the nature of the field. Although it is heir to a long history of the consolidation of science, shorn from the grounding culture, its unique understanding of psychology and culture drives it to reflect on its own evolution as a form of inquiry. The university setting allows it continually to merge, now with literature, now with philosophy, now with experimental science; and to re-find itself.

Psychoanalytic studies needs to define some aspect that is essentially psychoanalytic. Although its relationships with neighbouring departments might erode its distinctiveness, they might also facilitate a delineation by pushing back into it what is essentially psychoanalytic. Literature will treat psychoanalytic texts as texts, not as repositories of psychological truth; psychologists will look for agreement with their views of psychological development; sociologists will absorb its theory of groups and of mass behaviour; linguistics will analyse analytic speaking; philosophy will examine its credibility as a science or will establish what sort of science it is. What will remain - or emerge - as 'psychoanalytic' in psychoanalytic studies?

The essential discriminating feature - what stands out as its way of knowing - is the evanescent transferential moment. In this respect it cannot be absorbed into other fields. Similarities, however, can be found. The analytic process might be the best controlled

---

[2] On the early delineation of an empirical field of the study of the mind, see Figlio, K (1975), 'Theories of perception and the physiology of mind in the late eighteenth century', History of Science 13: 177-212.

setting for the tracking of such moments, but it is not the only setting. The question is whether or not there is an approach, applicable to any subject, called 'thinking psychoanalytically'. The same question could be asked of other fields: is there an approach, applicable to any field, called 'thinking historically', or philosophically, or scientifically? For history, it might be the authorship of stories in which other people appear as actors. That would be why history must be orientated towards the past, even in the case of contemporary history. It would have to sustain the illusion of authorship of a finished story in the mind of the historian. No matter how much the story is revised by historical scholarship, it is not an open story.[3]

Perhaps for psychoanalysis, an essential way of thinking might follow from a strict concept of the unconscious; perhaps from Freud's early observation that one had to understand the unconscious as one would another person. From such an notion comes the idea that only someone else can perceive one's unconscious, upon which both the idea of the transference and of the unconscious dimension of social processes can be built. The key theme, no matter how it is approached, is 'thinking psychoanalytically'.

From a psychoanalytic point of view, conscious utterances and claims to knowledge are also vehicles for unconscious expression and communication. Given the otherness of the unconscious, neighbouring disciplines in the university become vehicles for the expression and communication of these unconscious aspects of each other. Together they build a community in which, if it could be noticed, there would be a clear unconscious domain. Continuous interaction amongst fields is necessary to the healthy development of each of them. Psychoanalytic studies would share this process, but has its own object of study, in the unconscious dimension itself, including the appreciation of unconscious communication about itself from other fields.

I would like to develop this theme in the rest of the paper. In particular, I will follow a line of inquiry that has been prominent in the Kleinian orientation - that it is an inquiry into thinking itself.

For Freud, the fundamental processes of thinking come to light in their most serious disturbances.

---

[3] Arendt, H (1958), The Human Condition, Chicago/London: University of Chicago Press, ch. 5.

> It is only the analysis of one of the affections which we call the narcissistic psychoneuroses that promises to furnish us with conceptions through which the enigmatic Ucs. will be brought more within our reach and, as it were, made tangible.[4]

And he implies that the transference reveals the nature of the thinking process, in terms of a disorder that severs, in schizophrenia, the use of words from their referents. Speaking about a male patient who was preoccupied with blackheads, he said:

> Pressing out the content of the blackheads is clearly to him a substitute for masturbation. The cavity which then appears owing to his fault is the female genital. i.e. the fulfilment of the threat of castration...This substitutive formation has, in spite of its hypochondriachal character, considerable resemblance to a hysterical conversion; *and yet we have a feeling that something different must be going on here, that a substitutive formation such as this cannot be attributed to hysteria, even before we can say in what the difference consists.*[5]

For Freud's patient, words did not refer to anything outside themselves: they were things in themselves. The link between the cavity left from pressing out a blackhead and the female genital lay not in any similarity, but in the word itself. The word *could* have referred to either a pore or a genital, but in reality was just a word. Everything to which it might have referred, every metaphoric or creative use, was left unnoticed, unused, non-existent. Words, like Schreber's paranoiac fantasies, were objects from which a new world might be built after a psychic catastrophe, but they remained a private omnipotent phantasy.[6]

The sensitivity to the difference between words that engage and articulate a reality outside themselves and words that are omnipotent fabrications is a psychoanalytic sensitivity, a feature of the transference in the narcissistic psychoneuroses. Freud said he *could* feel the difference between a hysterical presentation, which would have mimetically portrayed his patient's castration anxiety in an identification of an enlarged pore with a vagina, and a schizo-

---

[4] Freud, Sigmund (1915), 'The unconscious', SE, XIV, pp. 159-215; p. 196.
[5] Freud, 'The unconscious', p. 200; my emphasis.
[6] Freud, (1911) 'Psycho-Analytic notes on an autobiographical account of a case of paranoia (dementia paranoides)' [Schreber], SE, XII, pp. 1-82., Pt III.

phrenic presentation, in which a word was a thing. That is a methodological point. I will return to it, to argue that thinking psychoanalytically means disturbing adjacent disciplines with a new method.

First, let us return to the comparison of normal and schizophrenic thinking: the former using words as signs and symbols, referring to something outside themselves; the latter using words as objects. Conceptual systems can be built from either kind of words.

For Freud:

> When we think in abstractions there is a danger that we may neglect the relations of words to unconscious thing-presentations, and it must be confessed that the expression and content of our philosophising then begins to acquire an unwelcome resemblance to the mode of operation of schizophrenics. We may, on the other hand, attempt a characterisation of the schizophrenics mode of thought by saying that he treats concrete things as though they were abstract.[7]

Freud suggests that philosophical thinking might detach itself from an external reality and become a symptomatic presentation amenable to psychoanalytic understanding.[8] In general, he thought that philosophers tended to stand back from empirical reality, and either hive off the notion of an unconscious into a mystical dimension or dismiss it by identifying the mental realm with consciousness and asserting that, by definition, an unconscious could not be mental. In this quotation he implies that philosophy is thinking in action, the mind displaying, analysing and theorising its own processes; and that its thinking tends towards schizophrenic thinking.

It would not be his only example of theory as delusion; nor did he dismiss it. Indeed Freud saw in 'endopsychic perception' a proto-theory of psychological functioning, which could be articulated by psychoanalysis. Endopsychic perception refers to an immediate awareness and articulation by the psyche of its own processes, which, because it is experienced as external and objective, is also the basis for projection. He understood the animistic mytho-

---

[7] Freud, 'The unconscious', p. 204)

[8] See also Freud (1913), 'The claims of psycho-analysis to scientific interest', SE, XIII, pp. 163-90; p. 180)

logical view of the world as such a proto-theory (of unconscious motivation); also paranoiac delusions (Schreber's world catastrophe and re-building as projections of a withdrawal of, and an attempt to reinvest libido in the world) and Rat Man's speaking his thoughts out loud, without hearing them (as a proto-theory of repression).[9] In a particularly malignant form, which he called a 'delusion of observation', one's every thought was exposed to view by a relentless commentary.[10]

The implication is that psychoanalysis could help philosophy by showing when its thinking went off the rails; or, in the normal situation, by adding new dimensions, both empirical and conceptual, to its direct and indirect aims of revealing the thinking process itself. The same might be said for other fields, although philosophy was especially close to psychoanalysis, in that its theorising was a form of the mind's articulation of its own processes. The problem can be generalised: thinking and theorising; spontaneous mental processes and scientific inquiry; the obstacles faced by the mentally disordered and by the scientist - they all derive from a common core.

Bion described the problem in this way.

> The difficulties of the patient suffering from a 'disorder of thought' are similar to those that beset scientists, and others concerned with the establishment of facts and so involve investigation of the nature of the failure. The failure of patients suffering from disorders of thought is patently within the personality. Psychoanalysis of that failure is impossible without understanding the problem of the philosopher of science and conversely his problem is incompletely stated without the aid of psychoanalytic experience of disorders of thought.[11]

The objects of our empirical world are complexes of impressions, which are gathered together as constant concomitants and apprehended as constitutive of the object. The naming of that conjunc-

---

[9] On the mythological view: Freud, S. (1901) Psychopathology of Everyday Life, SE, VI, pp. 258-9; SE, XII [Schreber], Pt III; (1909) 'Notes upon a case of obsessional neurosis' [Rat Man], SE, X, pp. 151-249; pp. 164, 231-2.

[10] Freud. S (1914) 'On narcissism: an introduction', SE, XIV, pp. 67-102; pp. 95-7.

[11] Bion, W (1962) Learning From Experience. London: Heinemann; Karnac, 1984, p. 66.

tion defines the object: whether it be 'daddy', as the child's definition of an object that derives from a conjunction of features, and then subsumes them; or 'chair'; or an object of scientific inquiry. In every case, a specific situation becomes salient when it is informed by a proto-concept, and forms an object that has some stability in the mind. The conceptualisation involves an abstraction from the constant concomitants, and whether as a name of an object or as a theory, stands apart from the sense data or other particularities that are gathered into the name or the theory. If that were not the case, the name/theory would become the same as the elements that make up the object: words would be things, and abstraction would not be possible (or, as quoted above, from Freud, there would be a strange kind of abstractness, in which words immediately elicited other words, not as theories or names that subsumed classes of experiences, but as direct associations among themselves).

For Bion, the process of thinking can be thought of as an object: a psychoanalytic object, the proper object of psychoanalytic observation. There are two main components of this object:

1) the mating of a pre-conception (for example, that the breast satisfies one's incomplete nature) with a realisation (that the breast is offered and an emotional experience follows); and,

2) the degree of narcissism, as opposed to social-ism.[12]

When words equal things, there is no mating between the mind and an external world, no limit to an omnipotent construction based on the proliferation of words. Normally, every name - every definition - of an object is also a hypothesis, an abstraction from the salient particularities, which is also an idea based on a model: the preconceptions of the mind mate with the specific realisations of a situation to produce a concept that is also a fact, meaning a registration of a stable unit of experience. The extent to which this process is facilitated is inversely related to the degree of narcissism in the process of abstraction: the degree to which words equal things. Narcissism interferes with thinking.

---

[12] Bion, W, Learning From Experience, pp. 69-70.

Teaching Transference

The relationship between a psychoanalytic object/name/definitory hypothesis and the salient features of impressions, sense data, etc., which it subsumes, is as much the concern of philosophical analysis as it is of psychoanalysis. What seems the particular concern of psychoanalysis is the second aspect, the narcissistic element. Narcissism cannot be registered through philosophical analysis, but appears in the transference.

It was narcissism that, at first, stymied the deeper psychoanalytic investigation of the mind. In Freud's view, the libidinal investment in the ego - characteristic of the narcissistic neuroses - ran counter to forming a transference. Unlike the case of the transference neuroses, in which libido readily reinvested other objects, including the analyst, the investigator of the narcissistic neuroses was deprived of the essential observational vantage point.

> In the case of schizophrenia ... , we have been driven to the assumption that after the process of repression the libido that has been withdrawn does not seek a new object, but retreats into the ego; that is to say, that here the object-cathexes are given up and a primitive objectless condition of narcissism is re-established. The incapacity of these patients for transference (so far as the pathological process extends)...seem[s] to agree excellently with the assumption that their object-cathexes have been given up.[13]

It was precisely this apparently withdrawn narcissistic situation, in which no transference could form, that British psychoanalysts in the Kleinian tradition studied in detail. They found that the withdrawn apathetic state actually expressed a most intense transference, but of a peculiar kind. It was as if the self, or part of it, took up residence in the object, and that the inward-directed attention only seemed detached from external reality, as observed from the outside. From inside the transference, the self-in-the-object had devoured the object in love and was dominating it to the minutest level in hate and fear.

Herbert Rosenfeld described the situation with such a patient as follows.

> [A]s soon as the schizophrenic approaches *any* object in love or hate he seems to become confused with this object,

---

[13] Freud, 'The unconscious', pp. 196-7)

and this is due not only to identification by introjection [the classical formulation], but to impulses and fantasies of entering inside the object with the whole or parts of himself in order to control it. Melanie Klein has suggested the term 'projective identification' for these processes. Projective identification, which is complementary to introjection of the object, throws some light on the infant's difficulty in distinguishing between the 'me' and the 'not me', and it explains a number of phenomena which are commonly called auto-erotic or narcissistic.[14]

In Bion's definition of a psychoanalytic object, the process of knowing such an object is inversely related to narcissism. Now we can see that narcissism expresses itself in an intense transference, established partly on the basis of projective identification, and 'observed' by the investigator as an experience of an in-dwelling presence or of self-consciousness.

Psychoanalytic studies is not concerned with understanding and treating patients, but it is concerned with thinking psychoanalytically and with contributing to thinking in general. If, as Bion says, the problems that beset the scientist are the same as those that burden a patient struggling with a psychosis, then the investigation of psychosis is the same, at root, as the investigation of any thinking process in any field. Disciplines that do not seek to define an external reality of nature and establish facts about it, such as philosophy or literature; or that take human endeavour as their object, such as history and law; share with psychoanalysis the aim of revealing the workings of the mind to itself. What marks out psychoanalysis, and therefore psychoanalytic studies in a university, is that it takes the very process of discovery to be at the same time a fabrication: not a fancy, but a form of self-creation driven by the narcissistic need to be the author of creation, including self-creation.

The process of thinking - the constitution of the psychoanalytic object - comprises this duality. As a duality constitutive of the thinking process, it becomes observable in the living moment of psychoanalytic observation, that is, in the transference. It is not a matter of the theory of the transference, but of the observation of

---

[14] Rosenfeld, H (1952) 'Transference-phenomena and transference-analysis in an acute catatonic schizophrenic patient', in Psychotic States: a Psychoanalytical Approach. London: Hogarth, 1965; Karnac, 1982, pp. 104-16; p. 106.

the evanescent moments in which the movements between narcissism and social-ism occur. So, although psychoanalytic studies may not be concerned with treating patients or with the theories and techniques of the psychoanalytic process, it is concerned with the transference.

Does this examination of the problem posed to psychoanalytic inquiry by narcissism, and the deeper observation of mental processes that followed from it, throw any light on the original theme of this paper - the place of psychoanalytic studies in the university? I have stayed away from the contribution of psychoanalytic theory to other fields: to the understanding of painting, drama, group behaviour, history, politics, biography, etc.; and also from the theoretical contribution of other fields to psychoanalysis. They are important, in that they supply additional models, but they do not distinguish psychoanalytic knowledge from any other kind of knowledge. I have focused instead on the notion of 'thinking psychoanalytically' - the doing of it, as well as the idea itself - in order to emphasise what the field has in common in itself, which exceeds the attraction of any one orientation to a neighbouring field.

Thinking psychoanalytically may offer insights into teaching and communicating information and ideas, including ways of maintaining an awareness of transference in the actual process of communication. There may also be ways of sensitising oneself to the transferential aspects of work in a variety of fields. The Tavistock Clinic has pioneered observational studies, not only of infants but of social settings and even of various work settings, in which observations are reported in psychodynamically-informed small groups.[15] Psychoanalytic studies could establish a setting for a transferentially alive experience of inquiry and communication in the various fields that surround it.

One could take this line of thinking further: not only could the social relationships of work be studied psychoanalytically; so also could the work itself, especially in the case of discovery. It is in inquiry that the problems that beset scientists, philosophers and people suffering from thought disorders most overlap. They all need to register, gather, generalise and define information, and hypothesise about an external world. There are similarities in the way one welcomes a new fact, a new thought, a new model or theory and a

---

[15] Miller, L (ed.) (1989) Closely Observed Infants. London: Duckworth.

new baby. Psychoanalytic theory generalises from emotionally charged primal relationships, such as that between baby and breast, to attitudes towards the object world.[16] It offers understandings, say, to historians, of the attitudes, thoughts, feelings and behaviour of the people whose lives and situations they study.

For example, thinking psychoanalytically, in addition to making use of models and theories, could help historians understand their own approach to their subject: the setting-up and defining of the problem, the selection and evaluation of data, the generalisation and formalisation of findings and the communication of understanding. It would be an interesting experiment to supervise historical inquiry as if it were a clinical or psychodynamic-observational situation. Such an experiment might be most immediately applied to interpretive fields, such as history, law, art history and theory, politics, cultural studies and many branches of sociology; but, *a priori*, it could be extended to fields that seek objectivity in overlapping areas, such as psychology and linguistics; and to abstract studies such as physics and mathematics.

I have concentrated on thinking psychoanalytically, in order to delineate a psychoanalytic core of psychoanalytic studies. Reflecting on its future in the university, I would generalise this form of analysis. As I said earlier, there is a 'thinking historically', 'thinking philosophically', etc., and these other approaches to knowledge could inform our understanding of psychoanalysis. Similarly, there is a 'thinking physically' and a 'thinking mathematically', which might do the same.

Langs and Badalamenti, for example, have developed a formalised model of communication in the psychoanalytic setting in terms of physical and mathematical models.[17] They claim that a field of inquiry, including psychoanalysis, can best be cast in well-defined terms, approximated by well-defined models that are amenable to quantitative treatment. Appropriately to their project, they draw their models from physics. They characterise the communication in a session in terms such the velocity, force and cumulative work of an informational particle (IP) moving through a

---

[16] cf. Money-Kyrle, R (1961/1978) Man's Picture of His World: a Psycho-Analytic Study. London: Duckworth.

[17] Langs, R and Badalamenti, A (1994) 'A formal science for psychoanalysis', British Journal of Psychotherapy 11(1): 92-105.

five-dimensional space that comprises significant features of communication such as tone and narrativity. The result is a quantitative record of the 'effort' put into communicating, taking account of particular aspects, not just the bulk of speech.[18]

Each field has its own methods, its own way of thinking. The value that each holds for another lies not so much in new information as in the unexpected way of thinking. Thinking psychoanalytically involves a peculiar kind of self-consciousness, an alertness to the impact of expression - especially speaking - on oneself. Thinking psychoanalytically builds on the observation of the transference as it changes form. For Bion, a key observation is the change in the use of speaking. As a psychic equivalent of motor discharge, speaking unburdens the psyche of unassimilated thoughts, which it experiences as frustrating bad objects; but in the service of relating to an external world, it also communicates thoughts that have been digested and can be used to alter the environment.

> Clinically this [change] shows itself in an increase in the patient of a sense of loss when he is speaking. The sense of loss appears to originate in an awareness that the thoughts being lost are good or valuable thoughts differing in this respect from beta-elements [unassimilated thoughts destined for evacuation]. The analyst likewise becomes aware of a change in the impact on himself of the patient's manipulation.[19]

The difference between these two modes of speaking turns on the antithesis between narcissism and social-ism.[20] In narcissism, it moves towards an anti-knowledge, based on the use of speaking (whether actual verbalisation or an equivalent, in phantasy, such as writing) to eliminate the frustration of the gap between an impulse and its fulfilment. In social-ism, it moves towards knowledge of the

---

[18] For more detailed considerations of this form of modelling, see the responses following their article, as well as Figlio, K (1996) 'Science, transference and the unconscious', British Journal of Psychotherapy; Langs and Badalamenti, (1994) 'Responses to Burgoyne and Harris, the discussants of 'A formal science for psychoanalysis' British Journal of Psychotherapy, 11(2): 303-5; and Schwartz, J (1995) 'Is physics really a good model for psychoanalysis? reflections on Langs and Badalamenti', British Journal of Psychotherapy, 11(4): 594-600.
[19] Bion, W, Learning From Experience, p. 85.
[20] Bion, W, Learning From Experience, p. 70.

difference between a word and its referent, between self and other, between an impulse and the environment that might satisfy it. This process - thinking - builds on symbolisation and the creative linking of thoughts, which presents new opportunities for relating to the external and internal worlds, not driven by the need to eliminate frustrating, persecuting bad objects.

Bion has assimilated precisely the unobservable, unthinkable narcissistic neuroses, which Freud said held the key to the deep understanding of the psyche. What seemed lacking, and what Bion found, was the transference that would open them to psychoanalytic observation. At root, 'thinking psychoanalytically' means observing and understanding these features of psychic processing, which show its moving towards knowledge or away from it; towards an external world or towards narcissism; towards tolerating external reality or towards omnipotent phantasy. It includes building models and theories about these processes.

Psychoanalytic studies is not psychoanalysis. It does not maintain a psychoanalytic setting nor aim to treat patients. Its unique offering, however, is still thinking psychoanalytically: the models and theories of psychic structure and their generalisation to social structure are secondary. For this reason, the inclusion of clinical and related interests into psychoanalytic studies programmes creates an opportunity for the consolidation of the field. It is not a matter of clinical training, but of a psychoanalytic presence.

In the university setting, as part of a community dedicated to knowledge, psychoanalytic studies becomes part of its self-consciousness as it gathers information, thinks, theorises and communicates. It is not a watch-dog, since its own work is as much an object of study as the work of any other field. It makes a special contribution in making a special study of transference.

It makes another special contribution in emphasising, and hopefully demonstrating, the value of counter-transference as a component of the observational equipment. I haven't referred explicitly to counter-transference, or to the idea of transference/counter-transference as an epistemological unit, beyond quoting Freud and Bion on the immediate impact of a patient upon an analyst. It is sufficient to define it as a self-observed self-consciousness of the correlation between another's self-presentation and one's own response - a response that needs always to be checked and corrected.

Teaching Transference

Thinking psychoanalytically in the dimension of the transference/counter-transference is the core of the psychoanalytic process, but it has rarely been introduced into non-clinical settings. I referred earlier to the lead in this direction, which the Tavistock Clinic has given with the practice of psychodynamic observation.[21] Samuels has defined a 'political psyche', in which counter-transference operates in each of us as a capacity to observe the psyche-like character of social, cultural and political events.[22] The university offers a microcosm, not just in being smaller, but in its common aim of inquiry and discovery, and in its common location. The different fields are all in the same space, both literally and metaphorically. Here is a dimension of inquiry and discourse in which thinking psychoanalytically could be realised and, in turn, studied.

The models and the theories of psychoanalysis are also available, and in turn will be corrected by other fields: the Oedipus complex, castration anxiety, penis envy, the good-enough mother, the psycho-sexual stages (oral, anal, phallic, genital), etc. But mainly, psychoanalytic studies contributes a psychoanalytic presence: a way of thinking and a way of observing a particular object - Bion's psychoanalytic object - which is the thinking process itself, observed in the transference, particularly in its orientation towards narcissism or social-ism.

---

[21] Miller, L (ed.) Closely Observed Infants

[22] Samuels, A (1993) 'The mirror and the hammer: depth psychology and political transformation', Free Associations 3(4)(no. 28), (followed by commentaries by Figlio, Mayers, Papadopoulos and Shamdasani), and the commentaries by Figlio, Mayers, Papadopoulos and Shamdasani; (1993) The Political Psyche. London/New York: Routledge.

The Crisis of the Univers(al)ity and the Future of Psychoanalytic Studies

Attila Banfalvi

If we look at the latest developments concerning the relationship between the university and psychoanalysis as a relatively new discipline, we could well be satisfied in view of the rising number of centres or institutes of psychoanalytic studies in many universities. It looks as if this is in line with the usual career of a new discipline or a new form of knowledge in the university. However, we could be afraid because this wished-for development seems rather formal or superficial. We can see that psychoanalysis has not been able to conquer the heart (if there is one) of the university, has not been able to become an essential part of the disciplinary structure. One cannot imagine a university without physics, biology or history, but everyone (except some 'obsessed' lovers of psychoanalysis) can think about a contemporary university without psychoanalytic studies. One might say this is the matter of tradition. Some day, it could be said, psychoanalytic studies will have a relatively long history and then it will have become an essential part of the university structure.

I am afraid that the situation is not so simple. I am also afraid that a much harder fate is awaiting psychoanalytic studies.

If psychoanalysis, as one of the most important new discoveries or attitudes of this century, cannot fit into the spirit of the contemporary universities smoothly, then it could be assumed that the problem can not only be found in this new branch of disciplines, but in the university as well. If this is true then psychoanalysis plays an important role because it reveals some 'errors' in the spirit and the operation of the modern university. Speaking dramatically, it can in itself show the crisis of the university.

Crisis? what crisis? One can say that everything goes more or less smoothly in their own way in the universities (apart from the usual and normal financial problems), most of the members of these institutes do not feel any crisis. The academics teach their narrow specialities and collect good points through publishing more and more papers on the conventional topics. Heidegger writes of such a one:

> '... the researcher, who participates in research projects. This gives fresh air to his work, not concern with his science. The researcher does not need a library in his home any more. Besides, he is always on the road. He joins in discussions in meetings and presents his views in congresses...'[1]

Therefore the first part of the title is rather disputable. Or is it proposing another point of view (in some sense an abnormal one) concerning the contemporary status of the universities?
What about the second part of the title? It sounds as if it aims at a prediction. What is the basis for this prediction? How could anyone be so brave after Karl Popper to take up a prediction about any future process or event? Is this not simply a mockery? Or if we assume prediction to be possible, how can we avoid playing Cassandra? Or is it not so important? The point is the Truth: so should we not bother about the fate of this prediction is?

And as far as psychoanalytic studies are concerned, they have been introduced into more and more universities. So at first glance it looks an unambiguously splendid process with a grand future in store for the subject. Or can we feel some shadow behind this favourable situation?

I do not want to 'unfurl' my answers to these questions until the end of this short paper. Before I make a detailed (albeit within this narrow frame) attempt at the answers, I will give my thoughts concerning the main questions of the title is as follows:

1. From a critical point of view the univers(al)ity is in a deep crisis. This crisis is not at all new, and many of the great thinkers of this century wrote about it. They proposed some solutions for these big problems, but at the same time they were rather sceptical about the future prospects.

2. Psychoanalytic studies has had a special role during the last decade which continues into the present. It plays the part of a symptom. Psychoanalytic studies is the return of some repressed

---

[1] Martin Heidegger: 'Die Zeit des Weltbildes', [The Age of Worldviews] in: **Gesamtausgabe** Band 5., Holzwege, Vittorio Klostermann, Frankfurt am Main: 1977, p. 85. [my translation]

The Crisis of the Univers(al)ity and the Future of Psychoanalytic Studies

aspects of the contemporary culture in the environment of the university. Psychoanalytic studies as a focus highlights some special features of the precipitation of the crisis of western culture as it appears in the working of universities. The possible alternatives of the future of psychoanalytic studies will show, as a sensitive instrument, the state of affairs concerning universality in the university. We can read this 'instrument': if psychoanalytic studies can fit into the discipline structure then we can hope that our civilisation is able to face some of its own repressed features and allow or compel the university as the focus of the main outcomes of this culture to mirror this new situation. In other ways, psychoanalytic studies will be a metoikos, not an equal power among the disciplines. Being a symptom it should be presented, however, not as a wished-for thing but as a satisfaction with unpleasure.

If we go more deeply into the first thesis of this short paper we find that a number of great thinkers of this century found that the European university was in an essential crisis. The essence of this crisis consists of the fact that the universality of the university is lost.

The main features of the crisis of the universality in the contemporary university are:

1. The universal coherence of the disciplines has been lost. This means that every discipline follows its own route which is determined by the special methods and requirements of the sphere of production and does not keep the wholeness of the human knowledge to the fore.

2. The factory-like feature of scientific research. The research process does not consist of thinking 'deeply' into the state of affairs, but rather follows the stricter and stricter rules of scientific methods, that is to say, follows the normal 'ways of life' of modern industry. Briefly speaking, the main issue is not the thing, but the method; as if the thing should adapt itself to a given fashionable method.

3. The competition between researchers on a quantitative and formal ground. Researchers are interested not so much in the quality of their thoughts as in the quantity of their 'thoughts'. The main issue is the amassing of production as in the case of industry in general. The great honoured scientist, the wise man, has become a researcher who is a little bit more than a technician or an engineer. The researcher is not required to produce - on the basis of an essential understanding - new theories, but to produce countable and measurable facts. As Horkheimer put it:'

> The engineer is not interested in understanding things for their own sake or for the sake of insight, but in accordance with their being fitted into a scheme, no matter how alien to their inner structure; this holds for living beings as well as for inanimate things. The engineer's mind is that of industrialism in its streamlined form.'[2]

4. The hierarchical order of the disciplines, where the position of a special discipline depends on

> its relationship towards the image of the ideal modern science, namely the mathematical physics

> the useful or practical outcomes of the research, in other words, what can be used as a new technology.

Between the different disciplines there is not a free exchange of ideas and thoughts. This is because in the world of values the discipline structure of a contemporary university resembles not so much a ball where every form of knowledge has the same status as any other, but rather the hierarchical structure of a medieval society. In effect, the place of a given discipline depends on its relation to the ruling discipline, namely mathematical physics.

The features of the contemporary university mentioned above have a dramatic impact on the status of psychoanalysis in the university. This means that psychoanalysis - if it is faithful to its vocation - is not able to find a firm place in the university.

---

[2] Max Horkheimer: **Eclipse of Reason**, The Seabury Press, New York: 1974, p. 151.

The Crisis of the Univers(al)ity and the Future of Psychoanalytic Studies

This crisis concerning the matter of psychoanalysis was reflected in Freud's thinking. He could feel that the situation around the psychoanalytical studies mirrored the crisis of the universality. As he wrote:

> 'Psychoanalysis follows a special method in the research of mind processes and thought operations, which could be applied not only for the mental disorders, but for the problems of arts, philosophy and religion, and it gave us in this way a number of new points of view and interesting information in the field of history of literature, mythology, history of civilisation, philosophy of religion, etc.,. ... The fertilisation of these disciplines by analytical ideas in terms of universitas literatum would provide a tighter relationship between medicine and the disciplines which are summarised in philosophy.'[3]

When Freud discussed the theme of quackery and lay-analysis he hinted at the problem that the medical school which lays claim to being a university nonetheless is not able to fulfil the demands of this position.

> 'An objection was raised rightly against medical training, that the student is informed one-sidedly in the field of anatomy, physics and chemistry, which failed to lead him to the importance of the psychic factors in the different life events, in the illnesses and in the medical treatment. This shortcoming of the training then proves to be the physician's shocking insufficiency. And this does not only reveal itself in that fact that he is not interested in the soul and sick people's most interesting problems but he becomes directly unskilful at the sick people's treatment, on whom every charlatan and healing artist can make a greater impression than he.'[4]

If we look into Freud's thoughts concerning the possibilities of psychoanalytic studies in the universities we feel as if nothing has changed. Or as if the problems were mentioned by Freud have become even sharper.

---

[3] Sigmund Freud: 'Kell-e az egyetemen a pszichoanalizist tanitani?' ['Should Students Learn Psychoanalysis in University?'] trans. Sandor Ferenczi, **Orvosegyetem**, 1971, 17, p. 6.

[4] Freud: 'Kell-e ...'.

Teaching Transference

The medical university is not more universal than it was in Freud's time. Its main features are:

1. Contemporary medicine has a great contradiction: It deals with human beings with non-human approach. Since the 'human' always means something disturbing, negative phenomenon in the contemporary practice. On the level of attitudes the patient does not differ from other living beings, even from machines. So he becomes an object, and only an object. All of them are subjected natural laws, just the man a bit more difficult structure. A sort of holistic approach is strange in the prevailing practise. The physician who takes the trouble to deals with the patient as a wholeness that is to say as a human being with all the consequences of this fact, is a deviant.

2. This situation has come into being because of the double fact:

> modern medicine is based predominantly on a natural scientific ground;
>
> the organic attitude is the prevailing one.

All in all the practice appreciates only one rationality: the natural scientific one.

This problem was shortly but clearly shown by Heidegger:

> 'If Dr. M claims that psychotherapy could only be pursued in that way which makes the human being an object, because the therapy is authoritative here, not the human being's existence, and because therapy could be pursued when it is not other than active treatment with objects, that is to say, it is a pure technical issue, then from this kind of therapy healthier individual will never come out. In the case of such a therapy the human being is definitively excluded, and even in the best case he could only be a polished object.'[5]

---

[5] Martin Heidegger: FreudrŰl Ès a pszichoter·pi·rŰl, [On Freud and Psychotherapy] ed. and trans. Mih·ly Vajda, in: FilozÛfusok FreudrÛl Ès a pszichoanalÌzisr¦l, [Philosophers on Freud and Psychoanalysis] CserÈpfalvi, Budapest: 1993. 60-61.

The Crisis of the Univers(al)ity and the Future of Psychoanalytic Studies

This is why from a philosophical point of view we can ask: What is the difference between the orientation and attitude of a physician and of a veterinary surgeon? There must be a difference, and a good doctor show this spontaneously in his practise.

The basic orientation or attitudes of a medical faculty or 'university' towards the human phenomenon and true human knowledge is paradigmatic in a sense which is typical and fundamental or prevailing for any contemporary university. The situation is different only in the case of the arts and similar disciplines, which are in some sense deviant forms of knowledge. This is why these are not allowed into the 'high society' of sciences.

If we take a short look at some basic features of the prevailing orientation of the contemporary sciences (and this determines what counts as true knowledge in our contemporary civilisation) we can understand why psychoanalysis cannot find its place in the branch of medicine or other sciences and why it shares the fate of the arts and arts-like disciplines:

1. The project of mastering. This means that one of the main impetuses which gives the power for the movement of modernity comes from the anxiety of the separated and fragmented individual. The individual who finds herself or himself to be thrown into negative freedom feels insecurity. This situation has two striking aspects: the narcissistic, 'standing-in-the-centre' self, on the one hand, and its paranoid relationship towards the outer world, on the other. This individual with a narcissistic-paranoid attitude is in combat with the threatening environment, first of all with Nature. The sciences with their methodical approaches play the role of the heaviest weapons in the hands of the forever fighting European individual.

2. Quantity, quantifiability, exactness and lawfulness as main values for scientific approach. The project of mastering can move ahead like an army if it is able to count the movement of the 'enemy' and can make predictions on this basis.

3. The central importance of methodology. The coming into prominence of the method 'giving priority of procedures against

being' (i.e. nature and history, which is objectified in research) is an 'automatic' outcome of the radical division between object and subject, individual and his world. The method is aimed at building a bridge between an object and a subject which are split asunder.

4. The technological approach. This means that what is seen as knowledge is basically not a knowledge for itself but a knowledge which in itself a means not an ends, which can be used in a step by step process for mastering something else.

Psychoanalysis from its birth has had difficulties with the features of an ideal science mentioned above. Psychoanalysis cannot be pressed so easily into the category of 'true' science: the labels applied to it have been ranging from myth to science. But three main point of view concerning the scientific status of psychoanalysis have crystallised:

1. Psychoanalysis is not a science, therefore it cannot give valid knowledge.

2. Psychoanalysis is a science, but its scientific features are not evident at first glance.

3. Psychoanalysis is not a science, but can give valid knowledge of the human being.

If we make a comparison between the above mentioned features of the contemporary scientific attitude and the main characteristics of psychoanalysis we can find that the third claim seems to be the most probable because:

1. Psychoanalysis carries in itself an attitude against mastering. This means that the psychoanalyst does not find any object in the patient's world which should be conquered. In a favourable process the patient can get more self-understanding or self-knowledge, but there is no ground for supposing that this self-knowledge can provide or guarantee self-mastering.

The Crisis of the Univers(al)ity and the Future of Psychoanalytic Studies

2, Psychoanalysis has not got to do with real quantity, exactness or lawfulness. It does not count, nor create tables, diagrams or practise any kind of method which uses mathematical measures.

3, The methods of psychoanalysis are not true methods in a scientific sense. It is not based on scientific laws, not because psychoanalysis did not discover such laws, but because it does not see the human being as capable of being understood on the basis of any kind of law. 'For a psychoanalysis', wrote Freud, 'is not an impartial scientific investigation, but a therapeutic measure. Its essence is not to prove anything, but merely to alter something.'[6] As a practical hermeneutics its methods are always provisional, therefore it has no any technology. Probably the most excellent example of this attitude is that of Sandor Ferenczi, who had tried many different techniques until he concluded:

> 'So finally one begins to wonder whether it would be natural and also to the purpose to be openly a human being with feelings, emphatic at times and frankly exasperated at other times? This means abandoning all 'technique' and avowing one's true colours just as is demanded of the patient.'[7]

4, Psychoanalysis cannot provide any technology for a better or happier life, it cannot even guarantee a better adaptation (in the superficial sense of this word) to the social environment. Its approach is based on free self creation, not a technology which is itself a mastering project. For psychoanalysis, a better self-understanding can lead to a worse adaptation to the social requirements, which may mean for a given person worse functioning, but better existing.

---

[6] Sigmund Freud: 'Analysis of a Phobia in a Five-year Old Boy', in: Case Histories I, Penguin Freud Library Vol. 8, Penguin Books, Harmondsworth, 1983, p. 263.
[7] The Clinical Diary of Sandor Ferenczi, ed. Judith Dupont, Harvard University Press, London: 1988, p. 94

From the above mentioned points we can see the ambiguous status of psychoanalysis in the university.

On the one hand, psychoanalysis does not fit into the line of the sciences. From this point of view it can find its place only in the lower strata of a scientific hierarchy; on the other hand, it can reveal the forgotten features of our possible knowledge. It shows the one-sidedness of the legitimate knowledge structure in the university. This is why I said previously that psychoanalytic studies mean the returning of the repressed. The returning of the repressed always provokes a new impetus of repression. It challenges the prevailing structures to mobilise new efforts against this perverse phenomenon. 'Perverse', in the sense that it reminds us of 'an infantile wish', namely, for the wholeness of human knowledge, and on this basis the Renaissance (which was the childhood of the modern culture) wish for the universality of the university.

This is why I think that the fate and future of psychoanalytic studies in the university is unforseeable and unpredictable. It depends on the balance of forces or power relations between the repressive forces of the contemporary style of scientific research and the partly repressed romantic style (in some sense) of the drive towards understanding human phenomena fully - that is to say, from many different angles as possible. This supposes two different point of view concerning the educated individual. The first considers that the main task of education is to provide useful knowledge, which includes mainly a kind of knowledge that transcends itself, which has an aim always beyond itself and is 'practical' in the sense of being subordinated to the mastering project. The other holds that education is more concerned with providing points of view for approaching the world, a world including human being. This type of knowledge is not always useful in the sense of always having practical consequences. However, it does have 'practical' consequences for those of us who like and teach psychoanalysis and know its importance in and to our culture. We should appreciate the relatively new situation where psychoanalytic studies can get into more and more universities, but the main features of the contemporary cultural milieu do not show any great promise that psychoanalysis will soon be the member of the 'VIP' branch of university disciplines. Nevertheless, we must work to prepare a new cultural area - especially in the universities.

Psychoanalysis, Psychoanalytic Studies and Universities
Alison Hall

> '...psychoanalytic insight could only be assimilated through constant psychic struggle...'[1]

The claim is regularly made that you can't know anything much about psychoanalysis if you are not, or have not been, in it. This is a general statement made about particular subjects and as such insupportable. Everyone who isn't blinded by dogma knows perfectly well that there are people who can be in analysis for years and remain remarkably ignorant about the unconscious in general and their own in particular. Equally, there are people who have never been in analysis but who, as a consequence of their particular psychical make - up, know a great deal about the unconscious. So in and of itself the badge of patienthood doesn't carry any status. Something else needs to be brought into the equation.

There is however, no doubt that working in an analysis, with a good analyst, and with the proviso that you are the right sort of particular subject, will give you access to a transmission of knowledge not ordinarily available through education. In order to say why this is so we have to distinguish between the aims of psychoanalysis and the aims of education. The aim of psychoanalysis is to offer an analysand the possibility of a confrontation with the particularity of his or her subjective truth. This is possible via a very particular transmission to the analysand of knowledge from his or her unconscious. The analysand's speech incarnates this knowledge. This is not insight in the sense of coming to know a pre - existent unknown with a previously fixed meaning, but rather insight

---

[1] Nunberg, H (1975) The Minutes of the Vienna Psychoanalytic Society Introduction, Vol 1, International Universities Press; 'Introduction'.

as a corollary of the production of knowledge. Most crucially it is an insight which includes a lack of knowledge at its centre.

The aims of education run contrary to those of psychoanalysis. Education implicates fixity of meaning and the illusion of mastery associated with understanding. The power of description, theoretical formulation, models, causal links, facts, stories, myths, fictions - whatever constitutes the explanatory substance of educational discourses - derives from points of fixity, from gaps being filled with fixed meanings. Education always aims to fill a gap and is fundamentally predicated on the assumption that all gaps are fillable, while psychoanalysis aims to help you live with the inevitable gap at the centre of your existence. The built-in dynamic of the analysand's desire subverts the educational project while the requirement for closure in educational discourse forecloses desire. Thus are they antithetical.

In his recent excellent book on Lacanian psychoanalysis, Bruce Fink alludes to Lacan's critique of understanding:

> Lacan reminds his students over and over to stop trying to understand everything, because understanding is ultimately a form of defence, of bringing everything back to what is already known. The more you try to understand, the less you hear - the less you can hear something new and different.[2]

The reference is to Lacan's advice to analysts but the advice is equally pertinent for analysands and is linked to the exhortation to analysands to say whatever comes to mind without censorship. This advice - 'Try to understand less!' - is directly opposed to the dominant commandment of education - 'Try to understand more!'

---

[2] Fink, Bruce (1996), The Lacanian Subject, Princeton University Press, Princeton NJ, p.149.

Psychoanalytic Studies

If the defining characteristic of psychoanalysis is the transmission of a knowledge to the analysand from his or her unconscious, and if this is unlikely to result from the educative process, what then is the business of psychoanalytic studies?

In his paper on lay analysis Freud engages in varied discussions of what he thinks is fit training for psychoanalysts.[3] The composite list includes a principal subject - depth psychology - and in addition an introduction to biology, the sciences of sexual life, the symptomatology of psychiatry, the history of civilisation, mythology, psychology of religion, science of literature, sociology, anatomy, biology and the study of evolution. It's a fairly extensive list and one that arguably would be added to now; e.g. it would be difficult to ignore linguistics. Freud notes, thankfully, that his catalogue is an ideal. It may also help with its enormity if we consider that psychoanalytic training, unlike many trainings, should not be understood as something which is of a fixed duration and finite size but rather an ongoing process. The point of Freud's list is not to encourage analysts to become omniscient so that they can impress, though that would be no bad thing, but to provide analysts with the optimum basis for being attuned to the cultural nuances and associations of the patient's discourse. More even than this, however, it is a call to analysts to engage in an ongoing research process with regard to mental life and the theoretical formulations of it. After a century, psychoanalytic research remains essentially embryonic and yet the potential here is enormous.

Perhaps the most important point about this list is that there is more chance of meeting its components in a university environment than anywhere else. More than that, the research ethos of universities lends itself to the kind of sustained research work which psychoanalysts and psychoanalysis needs.

Psychoanalytic studies is an umbrella term which encompasses:

---

[3] Freud, Sigmund, Standard Edition, XX.

study of psychoanalysis as a clinical practice based on work with unconscious mental processes

The theory of the clinic. Of course, in order to theorise clinical work a relation to it is required. The missing element in the equation noted at the beginning of this paper constitutes a substantial research problem of this type and yet it is only a tiny fraction of work required in this area.

study of psychoanalysis as a science and as a psychology

Is psychoanalysis a science? What is its epistemological basis? Does psychoanalytic theory force a questioning of any or all disciplines where subjectivity is implicated? What status should be accorded to the unconscious in mental life and what is its relation to consciousness? How do developments in modern neuroscience relate to psychoanalysis? These and related questions ought to concern us in psychoanalytic studies.

study of the origins, history and development of psychoanalysis

The surface has barely been scratched in these areas. The important pioneering work of early psychoanalysts largely awaits research. Universities are the appropriate environment for this research and also the natural home for accessible archives of material.

employment of psychoanalytic theory and methodology in the investigation of cultural phenomena and production.

This is the area least hampered by the fetters of psychoanalytic institutions which may explain why it has seen the most productive growth in universities. Of course it includes much work that pays lip service to psychoanalytic concepts while simultaneously distorting them, but it is an important area of innovative research and student interest.

Whether the issue is about the appropriate education of analysts or a more general dispersal of knowledge about psychoanalysis and work with psychoanalytic ideas, universities provide the education and research environment where psychoanalytic studies can survive - the alternative is inward - looking, antiquated and small - scale institutions inevitably marked by a siege mentality.

Psychoanalysis, Psychoanalytic Studies and Universities
The current context of university education.

Intellectualism has long been treated with suspicion in the UK but a 'discourse of the university' based on rationalism, proofs and 'knowledge for knowledge sake' could be said to exist. Or could it? There are two current and related trends in Higher Education which it seems to me largely contradict the idea of a university discourse and may be better characterised by some other model of a social bond. The two trends which I have in mind both gain their influence as part of the generalised baggage of pragmatic superficiality which characterises US institutional culture and which is regularly imposed or embraced elsewhere. What are they? First of all the onward stride of corporatism as a business ideology which knows no obstacles - certainly not the university gates. This is exemplified in universities by the following developments: Vice-chancellors need not be academics - much better if they have a cool business acumen than a string of learned publications; universities are 'human resource' environments where 'income generation' is the most valued activity; monitoring, counting and auditing are done on such a scale that academic managers and course leaders need to go on accountancy training; a collegiate ethic is replaced by a corporate one and the race is on for commercial sponsorship; research output is measured in tonnage rather than academic value; litigation culture is endemic and anyone with their eyes open goes for the low - risk option; and the ivory towers are peopled by marketing managers, public relations officers and media consultants. Perhaps emblematic of the lot is the way in which logos ceases to be the Greek Word and becomes instead a collective term for the proliferation of ever more tacky trademarks.

The flipside of this corporatism is that students have become consumers, customers and clients. And this is extremely fortuitous because it dovetails very nicely with today's version of the pernicious humanism which has been the bane of much intellectual development in the post - war period. In education this humanism is supported by a powerful myth of Victorian education. The Dickensian picture is of authoritarian and doctrinaire masters who forced a brutal rote-learning regime and who really liked nothing better than an excuse for mass caning. The power of this myth lies in its ability to support an educational practice in contradistinction to it. 'Bad practice' equalled the agency of education residing in a (bad) master, 'good practice' equals the agency of education residing in the self. 'Good practice' in educational thinking today relies very heavily on a self-psychology so massively embedded in Western culture that it is rendered almost invisible. Student-centred learning, like the customer relations of which it is a poor relative, is characterised by hollow pæans of respect for the individual while simultaneously choking any thing which breaches its codes, like anything really creative for example. Of course I am not suggesting that teaching should not be guided by a concern for the student, only that the limitations of the self-psychology which supports much current educational thinking should be revealed. For despite its kindly tone (or possibly because of it), it masks a universalizing way of thinking which discourages intellectual activity.

The hallmarks of this consist, for example, in publishing a 'Mission Statement' (who reads these? who believes them?) , and formulating a 'partnership' contract between the institution and the student; aims and objectives are spelt out (who would claim not to want to benefit the community?); surveys and questionnaires persistently seek to ascertain the extent to which the student understands the process in which she or he is a participant and how much it is meeting her or his needs; assessment criteria are taxonomized; emphasis is placed on a self-psychology conception of learning based on acquiring skills, capacities, attitudes and personal growth though 'old-fashioned' substantive knowledge hasn't yet been ejected altogether; and teachers are encouraged to renounce or refuse any form of authority because it might seem authoritarian.

In case I sound like an impassioned Luddite, I should point out that the examples I give above are merely some among many. Different universities will experience many of the above and more under slightly different banners. It is a feature of these discourses that they can appear with a range of interchangeable banalities masking the same banal thinking. Or is it more like anti - thinking?

The great danger it seems to me is not that 'university discourse' is any threat to psychoanalysis but that university discourse is itself under threat.

THINKING PSYCHOANALYTICALLY

Finding an Ear: Reflections on an Analytic Journey

Gerald J. Gargiulo

What is worth finding, to paraphrase D. W. Winnicott, is what we have had a hand in creating. A simple sentence to the eye, revelatory to the ear and enticing to the mind. Looking back on my years of teaching and practising psychoanalysis, I am convinced that only those experiences that have these qualities are worth knowing, remembering and making our own. In the thoughts that follow I hope to address how such an approach affects our understanding of psychoanalytic theory, practice and training. Since psychoanalysis is a profoundly human and personal endeavour, I will attempt to do this by recounting my own psychoanalytic pilgrimage over the past thirty years.

It was in my last years of training at the Training Institute of the National Psychological Association for Psychoanalysis that I was introduced to Winnicott, in a course on child analysis, taught by Dorothy Block. Dorothy was writing her book So The Witch Won't Eat Me[1] and recounted touching experiences of her therapy with children; she spoke of Winnicott with admiration and sensitivity. I had spent the last four years reading most of Freud and a number of Theodor Reik's[2] works - the latter since he had founded the Institute I was attending twenty years before. Reik was prodded to do so by a number of students he was privately training and by the myopic and 'anti-psychoanalytic' stance of the New York Psychoanalytic Society. They were willing to admit this creative colleague of Freud's on the condition that he not train anyone who did not possess a medical degree - Reik held a doctorate in psychology. That Freud himself wrote The Question of Lay Analysis [3] to defend Reik against similar prejudices in Europe meant nothing to these committed Freudians. And so I began my study of psychoanalysis disaffected, and in the nineteen sixties, with some feeling of

---

[1] Block, Dorothy, (1978), So The Witch Won't Eat Me , Houghton Mifflin, Boston.
[2] Reik, Theodor, (1956), Listening With The Third Ear, Grove Press, New York is one of his most insightful works
[3] Freud, S, (1926) Standard Edition, Vol. 20:183-250.

being disinherited from the official branch of psychoanalysis. Luckily I received at NPAP a solid and deep training in Freudian thought and I was spared the delusion that there was one priesthood to which I was supposed to belong. My own background included a master's degree in theology; I had been a lay professor of religious studies at a college in Riverdale, New York - I knew well, consequently, the seductions of dogma. What more I needed to learn about the danger of orthodoxy was taught to me by Winnicott. But I have gotten ahead of myself a bit.

There was a sympathy, I soon discovered, between Reik's candour as expressed in Listening With The Third Ear and the honest, forthright reflections I found in Winnicott. [4] It would, however, take me many years before I would begin to grasp the significance of his insights about our human need of finding and creating, of teddy bears and things and of understanding culture more as a mirror of man's hopes than a jailer of his dreams and desires. In my reading, teaching, and reading again, it became clear to me that finding and creating, while descriptive of early developmental processes, were equally crucial for adult maturation and experience(s). Crucial, for example, for how we come to form and to understand the role of intellectual abstractions, i.e., theory. Psychoanalytic theories are personal myths of meaning helping to organize our lives and direct the products of our hands. Such an approach does not lessen their operational validity, it is merely meant to appreciate the place and limitations of organizing models.[5]

Prior to and concurrent with my psychoanalytic training I was, as I indicated, a college professor of philosophy and religious studies, both disciplines of internality and meaning. Psychoanalysis was, I soon came to appreciate, a fruition of these studies. What I had discovered about the teaching of religious studies I would likewise come to confirm in my teaching of psychoanalysis, namely, that in teaching theory we have the promise of keeping a cultural enterprise alive; we also have the possibility and the op-

---

[4] see in particular: Winnicott, D. W. (1958), Collected Papers, London, Tavistock Publications. The Maturational Processes and the Facilitating Environment (1965) New York, International Universities Press. and most particularly: Playing and Reality (1971) London, Tavistock Publications.

[5] for a further discussion of this theme see: Gargiulo, Gerald. J.(1989) 'Authority, The Self and Psychoanalytic Experience', The Psychoanalytic Review, Vol. 76 No 2.

Finding an Ear

portunity of killing it. It was Origen, I believe, an early father of the Church, who spoke of knowledge as going from the known to the unknown - a building process. How easy, however, to project the known into the unknown, proclaim our discovery as truth and thereby calm anxiety. Dogma. No need to do battle with the muses of creation.

Winnicott, and what little I could find of Sandor Ferenczi, spoke to the issues of knowing and unknowing. Over my years of study, teaching and writing I would, of course, read many others, most recently the works of François Roustang[6]. And while I could admire Reik's candour, Eric Erikson's insights and Roustang's formulations, it was Winnicott, in his unassuming brilliance and poetic imagery, that conveyed the psychoanalytic task. Without poetic imagery can we hear the psyche or understand the words before our eyes? Theory, as I now conceive it, is to be played with and mused about, otherwise we lose a broad range of our analytic hearing and foreclose any consolation as we repeatedly encounter love and hate, pain and confusion.

How rare to read an analytic author building his thought(s) not with the clarity of a blueprint but with the evocativeness of a Cezanne. 'On the seashores of endless worlds.' Winnicott would quote the Indian poet Tagore and then go on to speak of man, woman and child; go on to write of that fertile space between the 'me' and the 'not me' - that bridge which we all walk upon, a bridge which both analyst and patient traverse as well. Long before North American psychoanalysis would accept the import of counter-transference in the therapeutic encounter, Winnicott had written of how he had to allow a moment of personal insanity in order to understand that the male patient before him was, to his eyes, female. Projective identification? Maybe. Built, however, upon a willingness to be had, so to speak, by a patient, not to be always in the know, being lost with a patient so that, together, they could find a way out - a passageway to what is real and alive. For an analyst, like myself, trained in the sixties in American ego psychology's notions of psychoanalysis, Winnicott's thoughts promised a way of doing analysis which respected our common human need to be with another in dialogue; not locked away in discreet obser-

---

[6] see: Roustang, François, (1982) Dire Mastery, Baltimore, John Hopkins University Press; and Psychoanalysis Never Lets Go, (1983). Baltimore, John Hopkins University Press.

vation, caring, but basically untouched, by the human drama unfolding before us. Freud's most obvious, and yet all too easily forgotten contribution, was that we can not hear ourselves unless another hears us and tells us of that hearing. How easy to substitute mechanisms of the mind and transference enactment's for the profoundly ethical and existential task of working out personal meaning through human discourse and relationship.

Along with my reading, it was my patients who forced me to understand and put into practice the observations Winnicott was so gently writing about. Forced me to acknowledge openly what I had felt quite personally, namely, that there was something dead in just observing and clarifying; in fostering a regression, and presuming that gratification was what a patient was surreptitiously seeking, eclipsing thereby a patient's development lacunae - a developmental absence needing both to be named and responded to. Thirty years ago these were new thoughts, at least to my North American ears; today we act as if we always knew them. And in the glimpses of case histories which Winnicott, in particular, gave us a new paradigm emerged for working with patients and talking about our work. When I came to teaching technique and theory I found, likewise, that I was using one case study, in particular, to convey new entries to the soul. Although I have spoken and written of this case elsewhere, I would like to summarize it again since I have found, like Reik and Winnicott, that it is in self-revelation as well as self-reflection that psychoanalysis is best conveyed. [7] Such an approach also helps lessen the perpetuation of what Reik referred to as psychoanalyese; an arcane, special language - more attuned to academic self-awareness than interpersonal reality.

Gary was a quiet man who seemed particularly out of place in the busyness of mid-Manhattan. He was, as I remember him, both innocent and bewildered; he was hardly able to articulate why he was in my office at all. As for myself I felt not only some concern, but protective of this unknown stranger. (I was puzzled by my feeling responses.) He was a carpenter, he said, as well as a political-Marxist activist. He spoke of his father who had left the family many years ago and of his mother in such distant terms that I was barely able to sense their presence. He grew up in a country farm

---

[7] Gargiulo, Gerald J. 'The Autobiography of Humpty Dumpty', read June 1995 London: Psychotherapy Consortium Lecture.

environment, of Swedish ancestry, and had, just a year or so ago, moved to New York City. After work, except when he attended his political discussion groups, he would go to his apartment and either read or play the piano.

Gary was a likeable young man who had little, if any social life. After speaking of his personal history, Gary was quite content to sit opposite me, on a twice-a-week basis, and say nothing to my attentive ears. He would, occasionally, give brief answers to my generic inquiries. To my gentle reminders that he try to say whatever might occur to him, with as little self-judgement as possible, Gary would smile uncomfortably while conveying bewilderment as to how he was supposed to speak of his insides. After a few months of our concerned stand-off, it became clear that I was not handling the case well and Gary wondered if therapy was for him.

I do not remember when it occurred to me to ask the most obvious of questions; in retrospect I am embarrassed by its simplicity. I asked Gary, one session, what it was like when there was so much silence between us. And in a quiet, calm voice he said that he was used to it. There was, he continued, hardly any speaking in his household when he was growing up. No talk at dinner time and after dinner he would go to his room, play piano or read. Occasionally he would hear his parents fighting. When he said this it became clear to me that our work together was not making headway since it was repeating and replicating Gary's childhood experiences. That was why my relatively silent presence was not experienced by him as a possibility for self-discovery. Gary did not know, in practice, anything about personal communicating. The space between us was cluttered with a dead silence.

If Gary had no bridge to reach me, then I would give him words, as building blocks; I decided, therefore, to speak and no longer to quietly wait for his associations. I spoke of carpentry, politics, piano playing or whatever he might mention. Gary listened and ever so slowly he began to answer, not with the dead language he had used till then but, almost imperceptibly, with a growing presence of tone and colour in his voice and a desire to connect in his intentions. The therapy continued for a number of years after this turning point and ever so slowly I was able to lessen my obvious presence as he was able to present his own. This occurred, I now understand, because we had found a therapy-playground where we were both on equal ground and having found that place, both of us

Teaching Transference

having a hand in its creation, Gary was able, not withstanding some developmental turbulence, to grow.

Psychoanalysis is about a mutual commitment to honesty, about equality, about one human being hearing the presences and the absences of an other; it re-awakens both love and hate and re-finds memory. When Freud spoke of freely hovering attention he was not fostering an observational technique but advocating an openness, on the analyst's part, so that a patient could make use of him/her - picture, if you will, different persons playing the same piano. I had, consequently, to remember my own silences before I could hear what Gary was saying to me.

How does one teach such a technique? Can we? In defending Reik in The Question of Lay Analysis Freud spoke of the necessity not only of avoiding psychoanalysis becoming a chapter in a psychiatric text, but of the need to attract individuals who were familiar with literature and poetry, history and theology, with all the gifts of a humanistic education and culture. How else could one listen with one's insides - such studies are ear training for the analyst. How different is this preparation from that of having as one's first therapeutic encounter, a cadaver. It was evident to me that Winnicott's commitment to children was in sharp contrast to the medical model of therapy, so prevalent when I did my studies and for many years thereafter. In my own teaching, while never explicitly teaching child therapy, I would bring in many texts such as The Velveteen Rabbit[8] or works of poets, (I particularly like The Four Quartets,[9]) in an attempt to help the student analysts feel comfortable and competent in their own hearing, a prerequisite for their evenly suspended listening to patients. When this is not done, what I frequently encounter are students who have mastered the words only to miss the meaning.

What my experiences with Gary also taught was that one cannot subsume everything which occurred in sessions under the rubric of transference. Transference, we know, is a model to organize psychological material, perceptive and useful within a therapeutic context. But as a 'catch all' for everything it becomes both obvious and useless. Obvious because the shadow of the past is always with us and any act, thought or phantasy can be understood in terms of

---

[8] Williams, Margery. (196?) The Velveteen Rabbit, Garden City, New York
[9] Eliot, T S (1943) Four Quartets, Harcourt Brace & Co. New York.

Finding an Ear

its genetic determinants. Obvious because we are historical by force of the consciousness we have evolved, and to be historical is to be had by all the personal, intellectual, emotional and cultural lineages that shadow us. Useless, because to interpret everything in the light of transference is to miss conveying to the patient the contrast between personal responsibility, present relationship and past experience(s). Only in a patient's experiencing an analyst for who he/she actually is can one distinguish idealizing positive transference or its negative.

In this vein it was not only Winnicott's unobtrusive yet personal presence, i.e., the squiggle games, that helped me but similarly the writings of Michael Balint.[10] Balint was able to put into words what I repeatedly thought: that neutrality was not an analyst playing schizoid, so to speak, but rather knowing him/herself soberly and realistically and responding to a patient in light of that knowledge. How else is an analyst able to balance transference and present reality. When Freud asked for a commitment from his patients for personal honesty - the fundamental rule - he was interacting with a living person before him, not talking to an imago through a darkened mirror. He presumed free will, although he had particular difficulty with that formulation; he presumed free will in order to work toward what Edward Glover would so aptly call freed will.[11] That Gary struggled with interpersonal relationships and personal meaning is clear: that his pathology had its roots, its fertilization in his past and his reaction(s) to that past, is obvious. What is also true is that interpretation alone, without the unpredictable squiggle game of words between us, without the experience of my interest and concern, would have accomplished little or nothing. He had to find and make me alive in order to use me. He had to experience that he could be alive in the presence of another alive person. Creating and finding - simple to the eye - profound in its implications.

Finding and creating, obviously, affects how we teach, particularly when communicating psychoanalytic concepts. When I teach I ask the students to remember that their primary task is to read everything, to reflect, as much as they are able to and then to forget everything. Paradoxically, only in knowing are we free to forget. If we do not learn we are substituting personal narcissism for

---

[10] Balint, Michael (1968) The Basic Fault, Brunner/Mazel Publishers, New York.
[11] Glover, Edward (1956) Freud or Jung?, Meridian Books, New York.

intellectual training; if we do not forget we are substituting personal awareness for self-forgetfulness - for freely hovering attention. Having established these ground rules, I find it helpful to read a few lines or a paragraph of primary sources and to give a personal exegesis, as it were. I then ask the students to do the same. I am not concerned with how much reading gets done in a course as long as the students know where to find what they might have interest in. Without the students wanting to make a text their own, an author their own, without a student experiencing a necessary delusion that what they are reading is just what they themselves were about to formulate, without such a delusion any knowledge will be relegated to the category of facts, not living theory.

There is no such a thing as a baby, without a mother, Winnicott wrote. Likewise, no analyst without a patient. Similarly no objective psychoanalytic theory without the personal fantasy, the necessary illusion, that it works. Just as words have no meaning outside of context and usage, just so is theory dependent on personal conviction in order to be used, found and created.

We can ask, consequently, is it possible to teach one to be a psychoanalyst? Or, are psychoanalysts born, to quote Reik? Are they individuals who have, in particular, an unfinished dialogue with their mothers, to echo Harold Searles?[12] We know that an essential ingredient of training is a personal analysis and it is here, perhaps most of all, that the personal illusion of effectiveness takes hold; here, that the reality of the persons involved is most fully felt. If my own analyst, back in the nineteen sixties, had not been a man fiercely dedicated to social justice and acutely aware of social psychology, would I have been responded to in a way that made me pre-disposed to hear the psyche within a wider orchestration than individual defences and conflicts? Without such an analytic experience it would have taken me longer to find Erik Erikson, before Winnicott, and see in him a direct route back to Freud; although clearly with new societal vistas? More importantly, would I have had the experience that my thoughts were of value to him, that they were not going to be repetitively pathologised, were he not the person he was? At the end of my five times a week, four year journey, we stood on equal ground. After thirty years we still do; rec-

---

[12] Searles, Harold, (1965) Collected Papers on Schizophrenia and Related Subjects, International Universities Press. New York.

Finding an Ear

ognizing, however, my clay feet, as well as his. I had built a bridge back to my past which I could walk upon, sometimes run upon, and so I was more able to help others build theirs.

The making of a psychoanalyst is a complicated task. The teaching of transference, for example, outside of the experience of personal therapy is, I believe, most difficult. Made more difficult, I believe, by the fact that many psychoanalytic training institutes are modelled on an oedipal triangle - there are the powerful older fathers requiring submission to particular theory and technique in order for the student analyst to be admitted into the prized inner circle of training analyst or teacher. Of late, in my own readings, it has been François Rousting who has highlighted the dangers of masters and disciples; who has helped me think about the contradiction(s) of teaching transference in institutes which, in fact, unknowingly (?) exploit it. Whenever dogma is imposed, transference is exploited.

After twenty-five years of teaching, I have grown concerned about private psychoanalytic institutes conferring the titled mantle. An answer, if one can speak in such terms, might be take the majority of training and teaching analysts out of the protected confines of private institutes, teaching as they do for love of subject matter and for need of patients, and to bring this liberating liberal psychoanalytic tradition into the open market place of academia. Even at the institute where I was trained, where there is an exceptional effort made not to exploit transference by creating a special priesthood in terms of approved training analysts and control analysts, the spectre of the select still casts some shadows. All graduates, some taking many years to complete their training, are approved to function as analysts, teachers and supervisors. But all too frequently student candidates yearn for the powerful father - for the one who knows - for the analyst who has no clay feet. Consequently, they seek to know, all too often, who their analyst's analyst might have been; what ethnic and/or religious background they come from and where they stand in the hierarchy of the institute. Would it not be better simply to know if an analyst possess good character and a clear mind? These seem to me to be the only pertinent concerns; concerns which, I believe, because of the hierarchical power structure and financial factors, many private training institutes have not kept jealous watch over.

Teaching Transference

I have encountered a few training centres in the United States which are institutes without walls, so to speak. Centres where an individual has a personal analysis, takes a number of seminars, studies intensively with his/her supervisors and somewhere along the process becomes self-reflectively and, within the context of their teachers and supervisors, aware that they are, in fact, functioning as a psychoanalyst. Close to Lacan's idea, as best I understand him, of the self-authentication involved in becoming an analyst. Just as one's personal analysis must be the work of one's hands, just so is the understanding and use of theory, an odyssey of knowledge. There are no knowing others; we are all alone but together, intermingled as air is to lungs in that aloneness.

What we are about, then, we who stand one hundred years upon Freud's shoulders, is the finding of mind and the construction of meaning - perennially tasks for humans. The location of mind, as I have written about elsewhere, has more to do with Winnicott's transitional space than has been appreciated.[13] Mind is not some solipsistic entity to be jealously guarded by each individual. It is, rather, the playground of human culture and of our common human yearnings, needs and phantasies; it is, in fact, what allows psychoanalysis to be a therapeutic. The finding of psyche, when it is lost, is the psychoanalyst's archaeology. Only when we find ourselves do we understand our commonality, so that we can use language as a bridge rather than a self-soothing panacea. The experience of meaning, in all its shades from conscious to unconscious, in all its manifestations from dogma to personal myths, is the task at hand. Since it is only in the self ownership, which the struggle for meaning entails, that an individual can experience freed will.

Notwithstanding my concerns about private training institutes, when we celebrate psychoanalysis and its teaching centres, when we struggle to find ways to bring psychoanalysis to the worlds we inhabit in our efforts to mend the wounds of life, we are, in fact,

---

[13] Gargiulo, Gerald J. (1996) (in press) 'Winnicott's Psychoanalytic Playground' in Psychoanalytic Versions Of The Human Condition and Clinical Practice, New York, New York University Press.

Finding an Ear

doing the work of culture. Sacred in its human import. We are, of course, also finding and creating ourselves.

Some Assertions about Self
Joel Ryce-Menuhin

I have been fascinated by the opportunities the University has potentially to assess and teach theory in psychoanalysis and in analytical psychology. When Louis Pasteur took up his professorship at Lille in 1854 he remarked, 'Without theory, practice is but routine born of habit. Theory alone can bring forth and develop the spirit of invention'

Today both Freudian and Jungian analysts have come up with very little important new theory but here and there we have practitioners and teachers who answer Pasteur's 'spirit of invention'. In this contribution to the tenth anniversary celebration of the Centre of Psychoanalytic Studies I would like to theoretically defend Jung's belief in a self theory which Freud did not consider as possible. In that process I shall extend by conjecture Sartre's theory of the consciousness of knowing. As a misconceived self theory would be one with an incorrect conception about how theories and observation actually build and grow up in infancy, I shall be looking at studies of infant observation and philosophic arguments as guidelines (among others) within tight space limitations.

The identity of self is a basic awareness of sameness across time and space. Through breaks in this self-awareness during sleep or when conscious, we are made aware of self as a continuity in its personal distinctness from other selves and objects. Hume argued in his *Treatise* (see 1896 edition) that we cannot have an idea of self, since we know nothing but sense impressions. In Book II, however, he wrote: 'Tis evident that ... we are at all times intimately conscious of ourselves, our sentiments and passions...' He saw self as merely the sum total of experiences, but if the self is linked to what is commonly named the individual differentiated personality, it itself must change, since it is both partially dependent on physical and intellectual development and partially independent via its inventive initiative.

The polarity between self and environment is the subject of most self studies. Knowledge, including culturally acquired knowledge, may effect interpretations of this polarity. As Ryle suggests, it may

Some Assertions about Self

be almost impossible to observe oneself as one is at a given instant, but one can reflect on oneself an instant later.[1] We can develop theories about ourselves through posing problems and testing our conjectures. This is an ongoing learning process.

Frantz's experiments with five-day-old babies show that they fixate for longer periods on a schematic drawing of a face than on a similar non-face pictorial arrangement.[2] Dependence on caretakers makes persons very important within the objects of a baby's environment. Through others' interest in him and through body-discovery the baby learns that he also is a person. To be a self, expectancy over time of one's self extending to past and future involves a theory of expectation.

However many ways of acting that being a self may include for the baby, social experience will add to the sum of self-awareness. What can be said to be individual about an organism that is an open system or group of systems with atoms frequently joining and leaving these systems? The material particles and energy are in constant exchange through metabolism with the environment. To the extent that this is self-controlling, the organism is a centre of control. A baby is a developing organism as a body before it becomes a person in the sense of a consciously perceived unity of body and mind, or psyche-soma. The baby's knowledge of his mother or principal caretaker leads on to his need to learn what is part of his body and what is not. In time the baby distinguishes between persons and things. This knowledge is needed prior to his discovery that he is a separate self.

Underlying this idea is a principle of social cognition: that any knowledge gained about the other must also be gained about the self. Banister and Agnew, in a chapter on the child's construction of self, maintain:

'The ways is which we elaborate our construing of self, must be essentially those ways in which we elaborate our construing of others, for we have not a concept of self but a bipolar construct of self/not-self or self-others.'[3]

---

[1] Ryle G (1949) The Concept of Mind, London: Hutchinson

[2] Franz R L (1963) 'Pattern vision in new-born infants', Science 140: 29607

[3] Bannister D and Agnew J (1976) 'The child's construing of self', in J Cole Ed. Nebraska Symposium on Motivation, Lincoln Neb: University of Nebraska Press

Teaching Transference

Lewis and Brooks-Gunn observed the first two years of development in the baby and propose a division of this development into four periods[4]:

1. Birth to three months: Infants are particularly interested in other babies as social objects. Single action-outcome pairings are seen regularly enough to postulate these primary circular reactions to be differentiated.

2. Three to eight months: Means and ends relationships are established. The baby and his own mirror-contingency becomes of interest to the baby within an action-outcome behaviour unit of experimentation. The self-other distinction is not consolidated prior to the notion of permanence.

3. Eight to twelve months: The critical development is the permanent establishment of the permanence notion that enables the infant to have a self-other distinction. Plans, intentionality, self-recognition, independence from some contingencies all appear.

4. Twelve to twenty-four months: The representational behaviour-of-self begins and self-recognition is more dependent on feature analysis than on contingency in experimentation. (The child can recognise self in pictures as well as in mirrors.) A categorical self-knowledge begins with gender and age.

In his language the child uses complex means-ends and symbolic representation occurs. For example, there are sentences we use once and never construct again. Understanding such a sentence is more than understanding the sequence of words, at which one might initially fail. A unique experience is suggested, not a learned response to a former stimulus, which probably has a brain-process that is also necessarily unique. Brown, in describing processes involved with the child's acquisition of syntax, mentions the induction of latent structure as the most complex and finds this more

---

[4] Lewis M and Brools-Bunn J (1979) Social Cognition and the Acquisition of Self, Plenum

Some Assertions about Self

reminiscent of the biological development of an embryo than of the acquisition of a conditioned response.[5]

In general the self seems both to observe and to take action at the same time.

> 'It (the self) is acting and suffering, recalling the past and planning and programming the future; expecting and disposing. It contains ... a vivid consciousness of being an acting self, a centre of action.'[6]

Adaptation to the external world may be inherited and learned. Both forms of knowledge can have complex informative capacity. Inherited knowledge, in the unconscious and found in the genes (the genome of the organism), provides the background from which to acquire new knowledge. The idea that sense-data are the only entrance to the intellect ignores the selection of evolution: ten thousand million neurones live together in the cerebral cortex. Eccles estimates that some of these neurones may have ten thousand synaptic links, which suggests a huge potential including genetic read-out in the inherited background of the baby.[7] Critical ability, in the sense of knowledge as the object of knowing or that' which is known or made known' (*Oxford English Dictionary*), leads to hypothesis and conjectural knowledge. Looking at an object causes an experience of sensation, but one then queries the problem of what it is. Man is constantly required to infer that other higher vertebrates have achieved conscious awareness in their decisions about interpersonal behaviour towards himself. Husserl argues that the one indubitable fact in human psychology is that of consciousness. Knowing demands a knower.[8] Just as there is no consciousness without an object, so is there also none without a subject. 'All knowing is consciousness of knowing'.[9]

Sartre proposes three knowings, to which I will add a fourth. He describes these as the normal extent of regressive comprehension;

---

[5] Brown R (1965) Social Psychology, New York: Macmillan

[6] Popper K R and Eccles J C (1977) The Self and Its Brain, Springer-Verlag

[7] Eccles J C (1964) The Physiology of Synapses, New York: Academic

[8] Husserl (1948) Experience and Judgement, London : Routledge & Kegan Paul

[9] Sartre J-P (1956) Being and Nothingness, New York: Philosophical Library

for example, 'I knew that I knew that I knew!' This first knowing is the phenomenological knowing of whatever the object is (realisation). The second follows in the knowing of the first knowing (memory via recovery and recall). The third knowing is a reflexive consciousness of consciousness, or knowing that one knows the first knowing. This third level of knowing is no longer a summation process. But as Sartre argues: 'Consciousness of self is not dual. If we wish to avoid an infinite regress, there must be an immediate, non-cognitive relation of the self to itself.'

In my view there is a fourth knowing, or a consciousness in which knowing is not known or transformed to cognitive knowing. If behaviour does not become an object of another behaviour by the same actor it is less than conscious or unconscious, but one can none the less speak of it as a knowing, or at least as a ground of knowing. This fourth level, a ground of knowing or being, is not a higher level of cognitive judgement but may relate to a ground of self-experience that intuitively includes unconscious and conscious self-integrates in its psychological resonance. Both Jung and Fordham have clinically elaborated a possible psychotic core of experiential influence of the self, thought of not only empirically but experientially as 'beyond experience', that is, in the totality-of-self.

My theory of a fourth level of knowing that is not dual or cognitive clarifies the sense that every experience is a partial experience of mind's total nature and activity, or totality-of-self. This fourth level senses that mind has attended to only a part of the whole of the ground of knowing and therefore recognises totality, which is known to be greater than the fullest active attention. This can be compared to Fordham's sense of the ego at its fullest awareness as remaining only a part of the self, never equalling it. This is sensed non-cognitively in the manner of my fourth level of knowing. When Sartre stopped at three levels of knowing he remained unaware of the further resonance that part-knowing indicates as a further parameter at the threshold level of that which is beyond the apprehension of the partial.

Instead of a hypothesis that our mind is a stream of experiences and the self only a summation of these as a functionally unified system of responses, I would argue that our minds focus active attention incorporating a selection programme which is adjusted to the repertoire of behavioural responses available but is not based on a mere summation of these.[10] Rather, the adjustment of behavioural response is based on an experimental 'validity' of knowing that has been apprehended by levels three (Sartre) and four (Ryce-Menuhin) indicated above. For example, if we look at Penfield's stimulation of the cortex in his patients, this stimulation enabled them to relive past experience while they retained full awareness of their body localisation as they lay on an operating table.[11] The patients reported that they maintained a conscious awareness of self while the perceptual experience of the past was restimulated. The central nervous system apparently steers the organism in an attempt both to relate to biologically relevant environmental aspects and to devolve some tasks to a hierarchically lower unconscious integration.

The individual organism, unique genetically and experientially with a long evolution of the central nervous system contained within it, must, in a unified or self-conscious and self-reflective way, use its own germ plasm linked to its own brain's connections to conscious/unconscious processes in its own descriptive function of language, This is the uniqueness or self of individuals, built up through the long evolution of human individuation.

Self includes both dispositions and expectations. Dispositions to recall to consciousness give continuity to the self via memory, and dispositions to behave unconsciously contain inbuilt expectations (Jung's archetypal theory) as well as inborn reactions and responses such as the new-born baby's expectation of being fed. Psychologically and genetically this knowledge is *a priori*: prior to all observational experience. Observation tends to be selective and presupposes similarity or its opposite. It also tends towards classification. This leads to an adoption of a frame of reference, to expectations and to formulations within theory.

I question the idea that science proceeds from observation to theory, rather than testing theory against observation, because although it is true that a particular hypothesis is designed to explain some preceding observations, the need for explanation invents new hypotheses and, expecting to find regularities, imposes them onto

---

[10] Skinner B F (1953) Science and Human Behaviour, New York: Macmillan

[11] Penfield W (1958) 'The excitable cortex in conscious man', Sherrington Lectures 5, Liverpool: Liverpool University Press

experience. Theoretical framework needs constant reassessment. Conjecture and refutation, rather than the preservation of current dogma, can be traced back as a method to Hellenic tradition and to Thales. A principle that emerges in Popper's work (1959, 1963, 1966, 1977) is that the criteria of demarcation for scientific theories are testability and falsifiability.[12]

The logical validity in repetition based upon similarity, or the inductive method, has been successfully refuted by Hume: instances of which we have no experience cannot logically be claimed to have to resemble those of which we have had experience. This questions reliance on statistical probability as all inclusive proof of any behavioural tendency. Habit does not originate in repetition: walking or speaking begin independently of repetition, before it can play any part.

Repetition is not perfect sameness for several interpreters: each is repetition-for-us if it is based on similarity-for-us. A giraffe and I might not experience a repetition as the same sameness because the giraffe and I would each have a certain point of view! If, logically, a point of view (such as a system of interests, assumptions, anticipations and expectations) must precede the decision that a repetition has been made, then the point of view is not merely the result of repetition, because it existed independently before the repetition. So induction, or a passive waiting for repetitions to impose regularities on us, is replaced by a theory of trial and error and the search for 'similarities-for-us'. Scientific theories are therefore inventions rather than a digest of observations, put forward for trial to learn if they oppose observations in a decisive way. This would presuppose a self rather than support an idea of building a self through regularities. Such a critical attitude enables the survival-of-the fittest theory at a given period in scientific history and, if an inadequate hypothesis is eliminated, the survival of science as such, as it can classify all theory as conjecture of tentative hypothesis. Empirical test and evidence can falsify by deductive inference but not by inductive interference, since no observation or

---

[12] Popper K R (1959) The Logic of Scientific Discovery, London: Hutchinson; (1963) Conjecture and Refutations, London: Routledge & Kegan Paul; (1965) Of Clouds and Clocks, Oxford: Oxford University Press; Popper K R and Eccles J C (1977) The Self and Its Brain, Springer-Verlag

Some Assertions about Self

experiment can give more than a finite number of repetitions. Statements of laws - for example B depends on A - always transcend possible empirical evidence. In general science accepts a theory as long as it stands up to the severest test that has yet been designed to refute it.

To balance these empirically scientific assertions I want to mention in closing that Jungians today are experiencing a revivification of self theory through ongoing studies of its spiritual symbolisation in which personal reality must be preserved together with its reality as symbol, or an archetypal figure of Self as a

> '... vision (which) can be perceived neither by the senses nor by pure intellect, but only by the Imagination that is its place of epiphany. The fact of spiritual experience thus described would exhibit an irreducible originality if we were obliged to refer only to a typology of mystical experiences such as is current in the West ...'[13]

---

[13] Corbin H (1960) Avicenna and The Visionary Recital, W R Trask, trans: Princeton, N J Princeton University Press

The Structural Problem in Phobia

Bernard Burgoyne

In any dream, beneath the scene of the dream lies a series of signifying terms. They are organised around a transference, a 'new edition' of something experienced in the recent past. In order to gain access to this transference, the mise-en-scène of the dream needs to be undone. This problem is exactly parallel to that of undoing the mise-en-scène that has brought a phobia into place. Underlying the scene of the phobic alarm is a series of signifying terms: in order to gain access to what underlies the phobia it is first necessary to have access to these signifying terms that construct it. It is the structure of these hidden histories that Freud is attempting to disclose in his analysis of Little Hans

Freud started his analysis of this phobia by distinguishing anxiety from fear: 'here then, we have the beginning of Hans's anxiety, as well as of his phobia. As we see, there is good reason for keeping the two separate'. The fear exists on the level of the manifest symptom; the anxiety underlies it, possessing a deeper and latent meaning, a meaning which the phobic symptom is trying to express. We have here then a relation between two levels: the symptom, without its associated signifying terms , is a superficial structure which stands in for a deeper structure. The network of pathways associated with the symptom leads onto a fundamental underlying structure of anxiety. The connection between these two networks - the network of displacements of the symptom, and the unconscious networks that generate it - is mediated by phrases that describe the feared situation and the object of the fear. It is in this sense that you can say that what gives rise to the symptom is put onto the stage by means of words. The drama that is then produced both presents and hides Hans's pain.

The phobia that Hans suffered from was fear of a horse; more specifically, a fear that a horse would bite him in the street. Just as Freud thought that a phantasy could be completely represented by a phrase - together with a class of transformations of that phrase -

The Structural Problem in Phobia

Hans's phobia can be represented by the following phrase: 'that a horse would bite me in the street - dass (mich) auf der Gasse ein Pferd beissen werde'. This phrase describes a scenario, a mise-en-scène, a putting onto the stage, that produces a story of the feared object and its properties. There are many other phrases crucially associated with this phrase, many of them transformations of each other; the problem of how such phrases and their transformations constitute the structure of the phobia is what needs to be addressed. The particularity of the phrases that built Hans's phobia became known to Freud only as he constructed the work of the analysis. But some of the particulars of Hans's family relations were known to him already: many of the details of Freud's connections with Hans's parents are now well known.

Freud's interventions responding to the phobia of Little Hans took place in the early months of 1908, but this was very far from being the first period of communication between Hans's parents and Freud. Hans's father was Max Graf, music critic for the Neues Wiener Journal and the Neue Freie Presse: he was no everyday critic, but a man of extensive culture, a musicologist who would publish more than a dozen books, in German and English, during his lifetime. Max Graf's interests were centred in music, but extended widely beyond this: he was a student of Bruckner's who found himself 'at ease in philosphy and the sciences'. Late in his life, he would write of his meetings with Heidegger and with Russell, and of the bearings of their philosophies on problems of meaning and the structure of relations. Well before the start of 1908, Graf had been taking notes on Hans's development and communicating them to Freud, who by that time was already a close friend. Graf's involvement with Freud, and with psychoanalysis, had started as early as 1900, when a friend, Olga Hönig, told him about her analysis with Freud, which was based, she said, on a remarkable method of 'question and answer'. Intrigued by any such method of investigating the structure of the mind, and by the reports on the unconscious that he was receiving from the woman who later would become his wife and the mother of Hans, Graf contacted Freud with the aim of collaborating in this field of work. He was successful in this, becoming one of the first people to join the work-group initiated by Freud which was to meet on Wednesday nights in Freud's house from 1902, before later being constituted as the Vienna Psychoanalytical Society. Freud set up this study group, it seeems, because he wanted his theories discussed 'from every possible point of view'. Hans was conceived three months before the start of these Wednesday meetings, probably around the time when Graf was invited to become one of the founder members of this pioneering group. The family friendships surrounding Herbert Graf - for that was Hans's given name - included Freud, who remainedan active and regular member of the family circle until the 1930s. Graf escaped from Austria to the United States in 1938, returning nine years later to Vienna, where he died in 1958 at the age of eighty-four.

Max Graf's son was to follow his father in taking up a musical vocation. He became a leading Opera Director, working with Schoenberg, Berg, Toscanini, and Bruno Walter. As a teenager during the First World War, Herbert had been sent to Germany, where he gained access to the work of Reinhardt in Berlin. He fell in love with the realism of Reinhardt's productions, and decided on the spot 'to do for opera what Reinhardt had done for the theatre'. In 1925, he submitted a Doctoral thesis in the University of Vienna: the subject was Wagner - on whom Max Graf had published two books and several articles before his son's visit to Berlin - and was concerned in particular withWagner as an Opera Director. With the end of his musical studies in Vienna, Herbert moved to Bayreuth to work on the Wagner productions there, working with Wagner's son Siegfried. In his interview with Francis Rizzo he recalled the phrases used by Siegfried: 'papa used to say', and 'papa did such and such'. He was fascinated by this Wagner connection to the father, but the low dialect the son had acquired from the father dispelled this awe, and 'helped bring me back to the realities of life'. Herbert worked also in Münster, and in the early 1930s split his time between Basel and Prague, before moving to Philadelphia for a year in 1934. It was there that he received the critical compliment - 'Graf has invented a new style of opera': the effects of his decision to follow Reinhardt were already visible in his work, which may have represented rather a decision to follow Max Graf than to follow Reinhardt. Whichever the case, these effects were maintained throughout the next forty years, and permeate the three books that he wrote about his operatic work in the United States. In fact there was to be a - sceptically intended, but - greater compliment for his work from the Americans to whom he had brought his new realism: 'Graf plans New Deal for opera'.

The Structural Problem in Phobia

After his season in Philadelphia Herbert Graf returned to Salzburg with Toscanini for two years before taking up a position as Director at the Metropolitan Opera in New York. He was to work with the Met for nearly thirty years, regularly visiting Europe; while in New York he set up opera workshops, and developed work with television. By 1962 he had settled in Switzerland, where he was to become Head of Geneva's Grand Théâtre, focussing his work, as he always had, on the problem of the real expressive power of the word in operatic production. He sought to summarise these researches in a motto: 'In the beginning was the word'. Freud had repeatedly emphasised this same Goethe reference in stressing the function of the word in his essay on lay analysis. The questions raised by both men converge on the same two themes, though with different solutions: in the field of general culture, certain effects within the field and functioning of words have 'meant an advance in civilisation' in Freud's formulation - precisely the type of advance that Herbert was planning with his new forms in Opera and with his proposals for a corresponding 'liberation' of theatrical structure. 'Look', he said to Rizzo, 'I'm a Professor's son ... a know-how man who believes that certain aspects of operatic know-how can be passed on to others'. In seeking for the parallel effect in clinical work, Freud tried to deduce from the functioning of words and phrases 'the delicate technique of psychoanalysis: the art of interpretation, the struggle against resistances, and the handling of transference'. Graf, for his part, sought to discover how words operating through the voice can gain access to what is real. The past, lost childhood and its lost loves, seek expression, but in Graf's formulations, he took it that this can only be done outside of the domain of reason: that this real hinterland is approachable only within the dream. The argument of Freud's book on dreams proposed a different answer to these questions: that within the suffering that is the gift of civilisation, there is an imperative to awake.

There is a weakness, a yearning. repeatedly appearing in Graf's reminiscences: 'Even today I can recall', he says in his interview with Rizzo, 'Erik Schmedes as the young Siegfried meltingly singing out his longing for his mother', and later, 'I remember', he says, 'one phrase from Siegfried - 'Ach möcht ich Sohn meiner Mutter sehen', and he asks 'why does it stay so strongly in my spirit?'. This 'single phrase' that lingers in his spirit voices a father's attachment to his mother in an address to his son. There is a reason why this

Teaching Transference

phrase remained for Herbert Graf as a haunting echo of his childhood sufferings: it bears directly on the relation of Herbert's father to his own mother, and on this father's relation to his wife. As we shall see, much of Hans's phobia constitutes a questioning of these relations, and a search for the reasons underlying his own anxieties in the face of the love relation with his mother. It would however take exactly forty-nine years - from May 1908 to May 1957 - before Lacan explicitly laid out solutions to the problems at play in Litle Hans's questionings about what he would lose in his dealings with love. The leitmotif of loss in what Graf puts forward as the predicaments of his work in opera produces an echo: 'we risk losing the true expressive power formerly in opera' when we have 'badly understood something that's fundamental in ... years gone by'. The function of the university, Graf says, is to transmit - the theatre, on the other hand, interprets the past afresh with each new generation. Reason belongs to the university, while 'opera is fundamentally unreasonable' - like any art, interpreting the 'innermost, inarticulate' emotions of the audience by a process that he calls that of 'crystallizing'.

In his interview with Rizzo, Herbert repeatedly describes his father as a man: 'a universal man... (he was) an extraordinary man, the most extraordinary (man) I've ever known'. He presents him as a man who could - and did- 'talk mathematics with Einstein', as a man who could enjoy a 'glass (or more) of wine, and the company of prettty women'. Despite this surround of women, what Herbert remembers as one of his father's most cherished objects is a book: 'a well-worn, annotated copy of Kant's Critique of Pure Reason'. This is the book that occurs in the memory or fantasy that Herbert retells to Rizzo:

> 'One of my most vivid boyhood memories is seeing him on the crowded footboard of a trolley headed for the Sunday soccer match at the Hohe Warte, one hand on the railing, the other clutching ... Kant's Critique of Pure Reason.'

A father with both hands so occupied has none left for the glass of wine, or the women. Sunday was the day that Max Graf would visit his mother, taking his son with him: so this father was a great man, but perhaps with some shortcomings with women. Herbert echoed too, his mother's initial description of psychoanalysis - the one that had raised the father's curiosity: 'Freud directed (the

The Structural Problem in Phobia

analysis) ... my father acting as a go-between ... (in) a kind of question-and-answer game'. This 'go-between' position for the father is what renders questioning weak; and it is hardly Freud that gave him this position, but the mother. When a child starts to question the insufficiency of what the father does with the mother, a phobia is in construction; the dialectic of this questioning can give him some answers that the father can not. With these memories of yearning and voices, of mother-love and loss, Graf continued to construct projects for work: for new forms of theatre, and for collaborative work: Toscanini in Salzburg, Mario Lanza in opera workshops in the United States, Callas in Italy. The extent of this work programme went well beyond the impulsions of a child's love, while it still remained ultimately attached to phrases andstagings that could easily express the predicament of his childhood fears. There is a story that when he was in New York Herbert Graf put on a production of Il Trovatore which is the only version of it ever produced where twenty-three horses come onto the stage during the final Act.

Love for the mother is the theme with which Freud starts his account of Hans's analysis. More specifically, he introduces the themes of love for the mother, of loss of mother-love, and of the corresponding function of the father in the complex of the Oedipal relations of the child. The dream that starts the material that Graf had given to Freud is as follows:-

> Hans woke up: in his sleep he had thought 'that you were gone, and I had no Mummy to play and caress with' ('du bist fort, und ich hab' keine Mammi zum Schmeicheln').

The term that Strachey translates as 'coax' is better kept in a form that refers to caresses and longing, and hence to the determined and desperate fight that the boy is waging in the face of the threatened loss of his primary, and most cherished, love. There is a verb present which already alludes to this loss: fortgehen. The transformations that this and other words are subject to build up the organisation that constructs the world in which Little Hans finds himself, and the reconstruction of this world is what much of Freud's analysis is devoted to. It is such words addressed to the mother - suppose you were to go away ('wenn du fortgehst') - that get him taken from his own bed into that of his mother. In the face of this, the father is somewhat dismissive of his own memory of these scenes: 'it was something like that: I don't remember the wording' - though this forgetful father certainly supposes these words to have got the boy into his wife's bed. The words may well be quite exact. Whatever the motives and outcome of Graf's doubt in this instance, his reports to Freud are generally such that enough of the wording comes through to allow the supposition to be maintained that a series of actual connections between words can be constructed from the material that he conveyed to Freud. This supposition enables the lines of Hans's phobic structure to be drawn.

There is another form of 'gehen' that occurs in relation to the mother: as she tries to take him out to where he might see the horse, Hans's 'will nicht weggehen, fürchtet sich' ('won't set off, and is afraid'). This is a version of Hans's speech, and so here also some reservation needs to be made, but there are other allusions that are more direct, and their effect accumulates: already there is in existence a series 'gehen, weggehen, fortgehen', and this series of phrases will continue, forming as it does, a framework for Hans's versions of love. The symbolic network constructed around transformations of phrases involving 'Weg' in Hans's case corresponds exactly to the series of phrases that Freud constructs around the stem 'Hof' in his analysis of the 'new editions' in Dora's dreams. There are structural parallels in the construction of a phobia and in the making of hysterical symptomology, as both the fear and the hysterical symptom stand in for something that causes them: there is a substitution. In the case of the phobia, Freud is clear from the start that the fear and the anxiety are separate, and that one stands in for the other. The mise-en-scène of the anxiety takes the form of the fear of an object, but how the standing-in takes place remains a question to be formulated and resolved.

Such questions of substitution and symbolisation have been at the centre of Lacan's theories from the late 40s; they had always been at the centre of Freud's work, and they could have been the centre of British psychoanalysis from 1916. The interest displayed by Ernest Jones in language functioning and symbolism stems from before the First World War, but any consequences of his wartime paper on symbolism were conveyed to the British psychoanalytical movement only by means of Jones's personal influence. The first serious critical assessment of this paper was not published until after the Second World War, in the form of Lacan's hommage to

The Structural Problem in Phobia

Jones, written in 1959, and constructed as a memorial to Jones's work. In this paper Lacan's criticism of Jones is contained within his claim that the proper grasp of symbolism is mathematical. Jones in his paper had appealed to his readers to 'reflect on the development of ... science' in order to grasp the characteristics of the development of symbolism. Lacan takes this appeal seriously, invoking the work of Bruno, Kepler, and Newton, in proposing that 'all thinking is symbolic', and that scientific thinking since the renaissance, incarnating the structures of mathematics, provides the apparatus by means of which human subjectivity can be located and analysed. 'Symbolic thinking', he says, 'has to be situated in relation to scientific thinking', and Jones's appeal to concreteness, Lacan claims, will never provide any 'true' account of symbolism. Lacan's theory has immediate consequences for the analysis of transference, for the problem of the analysis of the symbolic armature for which the transference is a vehicle. It is clear that the orientation that Lacan is constructing gives a very different view of reality from that maintained by Jones, and that the Lacanian option is not one that has been taken seriously so far in Britain. If Lacan's work were produced in the format of Strachey's Standard Edition, it would compose some seventy volumes: one or two of which would be taken up with the 'Seminar on Object Relations' given by Lacan a year or two prior to his work on Jones. It is in this Seminar - largely unknown in Britiain - that Lacan constructs an account of the structure of an infantile phobia, and he does so - as was his habit in those days - by means of an intricate analysis of the corresponding Case Study constructed by Freud. So these questions of substitution and structure Lacan takes to be presented by the castration motifs present in Hans's love for his mother.

The problem that starts the warfare of the Oedipus Complex involves the recognition by the child of a tension in relation to the mother and the father. Once this problem is engaged with, the ensuing anxieties are as much a function of the dangers felt to be present in remaining captured by the devouring love of the mother, as they are signals of the danger of being torn from this field of love forever. If we leave to one side for a moment the range of theories of anxiety that attempt to give coordinates to this predicament - Freud has several such theories, so too had Lacan - we find that here Lacan uses a specific theory to describe Hans's anxiety. Anxiety appears, says Lacan, at that point when the child can 'take the measure of the extent of the differnce that there is between why it is that he is loved, and what it is that he can give'. The nature of this anxiety however is not immediately the problem, rather the question that Lacan raises is what it is that structures the fear so that it is encapsulated into the body of what Herbert Graf proposed to call a 'crystallization'. This term too has a variety of ways in whichit can be used - one finds Stendhal using it to describe the structure of love. Lacan will develop the term in his analysis of phobia, but he will do so in a very particular way. The following questions now cluster around the analysis of phobia:

(i) in what sense does the symbolic functioning of the phobia have a structure?

(ii) what network can be appealed to in order to connect the phrases that express it?

(iii) is such mise-en-scène in any sense a crystallization?

(iv) in what way is Freud appealing to a structure that in this sense makes a geometry out of love?

In the Summer holidays at Gmunden, there was a phrase that Max Graf remembers well: 'das Pferd soll wegfahren' - the horse should drive off - with the father. This Weg stem now is part of a series of symbols that represent both the absent mother, and the attempt to absent the father - what Freud calls the question of fear of, as well as fear for the father. The fear for the father is also a question of fear of his loss.

The series continues:fortgehen/weggehen/wegfahren/wegfahren mit dem Wagen - drive off with the cart. What Freud calls Hans's 'wagon games' appear at the end of this thread; the wagon games, says Freud, are in 'eine symbolische ersetzende Beziehung' - a relation of symbolic substitution- to another wish. And it is this sym-

The Structural Problem in Phobia

bolic substitution that will explain Herbert Graf's crystal; and perhaps even the other way round.

The series of signifying terms continue, and in doing so form a network - wegfahren: drive away, carry away, cart off - Wagen dem Pferd: the horse's cart - wegen dem Pferd: because of the horse. Freud here even adds 'it must never be forgotten how ... much more significant (for children rather than for grown-up people) are similarities in sounds of words'. Hans throws himself on the floor, and spits and screams when asked by his father if he likes his mother's knickers (obviously, says Lacan of this display, Hans is not a fetishist); 'Hans, why are you lying on the ground spitting and screaming?' asks the father: 'Wegen der Hose' answers the boy - 'because of the knickers'. Wegen der Hose - Wegen dem Pferd - Wagen dem Pferd: Weg vehicles a conflict involving the father and the mother.

There is a phantasy that Hans constructs concerning his relation to his father and his father's mother. Hans is in a train at the station at Lainz, and travels home in it with his grandmother; his father 'hadn't got down from the bridge yet' and missed it. There was a second train approaching from the previous station at St. Veit, and the father subsequently caught this train, with Hans, and they both travelled home together. This phantasy of the impossible journey with the father in the train (after visiting, and usually leaving, the father's mother) continues the series of terms that traverse the crystal. As Hans attempts to find a way through the terms and pathways that constitute this world he tries to give himself an orientation: 'wir sind beide erst mit dem zweiten Zuge weggefahren - both of us only got away by the second train'. The 'Weg' term has continued its journey, and now the phrase is part of an impossible situation with the father. It is at this point, says Lacan, that the child is trying 'to take a step that he has to take, that is impossible for him alone', and where the pathways open to him are constituted by a series of dangerous points that relate his anxiety to the structuring of the world of his relations to the others. There is a need in this situation for a structure that allows him to workthrough these difficulties, these impossibilities, in more than an imagined way. Hans has a problem, and he needs an instrument with which to solve it: a structure of symbolic terms with which to investigate the relations with the father, and the father's relations with women. How it is that all of these relations are 'irreducible' to the deperately threatened love ties that he wishes to maintain to his mother will then be a problem that Hans finds resolvable in terms of the elements of his crystal lattice. There are a number of other threads: I will pass over Graf - G(i)raf(fe), though presumably Freud did not. But there are more terms in the Graf crystal: 'unter' is one of them. In the Lainz phantasy the father had to pass under the railway bridge; the station further along the line is called in full Unter-St. Veit; the street Hans has to walk out onto in front of his house is Untere Viaduktgasse; there is a constant switch between Unterhose and Hose - generally, his mother's knickers, and his own pants, the pants that have to be opened by the father so that his pee-maker can be pushed through, the pee-maker that is under the horse, and that he draws under the giraffe.

Freud's claims for the structural importance of infantile phobia are as follows: 'the neuroses of ... other patients could in every instance be traced back to the same infantile complexes that were revealed behind Hans's phobia.', and ' we find regularly that ... neurosis has as its point of departure an infantile anxiety such as we have been discussing, and is in fact a continuation of it; so that, as it were, a continuous and undisturbed thread of psychic activity,taking its start from the conflicts of ... childhood, has been spun through (the patient's) life.' These threads go through the crystal, along the lines of the surface of the structure that Hans the philosopher - as Freud describes him, 'metaphysicician' as Lacan reformulates it - constructs in order to resolve his problems. These sobriquets are not undeserved: there is an activity here which is actually precursory to science. Hans's problem-solving activity may be constructed in terms of myth and 'crystallization'; but the myth is what Freud calls a 'scientific myth', and it draws into its field the themes of Hans's loves in order that he can find a space there where some of them may be brought to a conclusion.

There is a scene where Hans is trying to get into his parents' bed during the Summer holidays at Gmunden; he talks about the older girl Mariedl whom he has fallen in love with, and his parents tell him that Mariedl should be downstairs sleeping with her parents - there is some inconsistency here, but parents are sometimes like that. It is his mother that Hans is aiming at, and he brings the terms of his crystal to bear on her: she replies in kind.

Hans: 'So geh'ich halt hinunter zur Mariedl schlafen'

The Structural Problem in Phobia

Mother: 'Du willst wirklich von der Mammi weggehen ...?... Wenn du wirklich von Vatti und Mammi gehen willst, so nimm dir deinen Rock und deine Hose, und, Adieu.'

(Hans: 'So I'm going down to sleep with Mariedl'

Mother: 'You really want to go away from Mummy? ... If you really want to go away from Daddy and Mummy, then take your coat and your pants, and - Goodbye.')

The parts of the crystal at play here are Weg, gehen, Hose, unter: these terms construct the context for a movement from the bed of the mother to the bed of a girl. His new love represents a hope for Hans - to escape from the intrusions of his father's opposition, to find forms of love that loosen his captivation to his mother, to find access to resolutions of love that are no longer threatened with terrifying forms of objection.

Love, then, is at the heart of things: the breaking of the love that makes up the 'primitive imaginary relation' to the mother is part of the body of relations that characterise the oedipal warfare in its earliest form. Lacan formulates a direction for a line of advance leading from this early captivating pole of love to a pole that more characterises 'successful' interventions by the father. He points out that one of the stages of this progression will involve a function of 'veiling, unveiling, and surprise'; a series of steps is necessary, in order to move through the castrating effects of the father's interdiction. These intermediary positions are described by Lacan as a 'series of mythical constructions' produced by the child as an attempt to give coordinates to his world and to the transformations being operated upon it. Hans is towards the end of such a series when he proposes a story to his father: 'You've got to be naked, and knock up against a stone, and bleed, and then I can be alone with Mummy a little bit.' If the father allows his own castration to be apparent, then the child can be with the mother without fear. There are many intermediary little myths - of Hans breaking the law with his father, of Hans constructing versions of what his mother wants, of Hans proposing what it is that makes a creature animate. This series of myths is in some sense related to the Freud-Graf crystal and its threads: in order to investigate this relationship, Lacan suggests relying on a 'method' - not the illustrious one

Teaching Transference

of Descartes, but what Lacan calls the 'méthode' of Claude Lévi-Strauss.

Lacan started his fourth seminar in November 1956. Earlier that year he had studied transformations of 'parallel' myths in the case of the Rat-man. As Seminar Four progressed, he was led to draw on the work of Lévi-Strauss, in fact on a paper published in 1955, on the theme of transformations of myths, and on the structure they need to possess in order to be capable of this kind of transition. Lacan is looking for an explanation for the particular situation of a little boy, but looking at the same time for a matrix which gives a universal structuring to this boy's experience. There is a strong tradition of the analysis of myth, from Louis Gernet to his student Jean-Pierre Vernant, from Marcel Granet to Lévi-Strauss, which sees the structure of myth as giving a form of social experience to the individuals in a social group: the world is understood in terms of this myth, and the creativity of the individual is constrained to be a 'legendary imagination', hemmed-in and given its orientation by the structure of such myths. In addressing in this way the problem of the social relations of the child, and in trying to locate the place of love in theorganisation of this world, Lacan borrowed a central concept from structural anthropology, one that we have seen alluded to before.

Lévi-Strauss builds a theory of the transformations of terms that generate the changing structure of any myth in its successive versions. This process of transformation constitutes an elementary structure that he calls a 'crystal'. The myth-crystal is used to formulate a version of the reality of the world, and in particular, to give a formulation to certain impossiblities. Each sheet-section across the myth represents one form of the myth; all forms are successively addressed to resolving real contradictions in the surrounding object-world of the individual. We have seen how Lacan sees the testing out of such impossibilities as the coming into being of the child's attempts to introduce the symbolic function of the father into the otherwise encompasing 'imaginary' relation to the mother. That 'crystal' is the appropriate term for such an apparatus is a notion proposed by Lévi-Strauss: the myth, he says, is a being made of words. Its structure and composition parallel those of crystal structures in the physical world - a discontinous succession of planes cross point after point of the crystal, and make up the body of the child's relations with the others.

The Structural Problem in Phobia

Lacan can now propose an answer to the question: what is the structure of a phobia in general, and in particular, what terms give meaning to Little Hans's fear? Lacan formulates the structure of the phobia in terms of the associative links between the 'key' terms constucting the phobic scenario; and he takes this to be identical with the crystal structure determined by Lévi-Strauss as constitutive of a myth. So Little Hans's horse-saga becomes resolved into the determining edges of a crystal. It is these lines of association that build the network of associations that can lead from the symptom of the horse-phobia to the underlying unconscious material constituting the oedipal anxieties in the unconscious of the child. The mathematics of the anthropology provides a solution to the problem of finding how the neurosis is constructed, and how its content can be assembled, starting from the expressions of the symptomatic fear. The pathway from the symptom to the underlying unconscious content is made up of elements taken from the points and edges of this crystal-structure. Any such pathway is what Freud calls a 'thread of free-association', or at some other moments, a 'logical thread'. All the lines joining signifying terms - including the line which joins a pre-transference term, with its innocuous meaning, to the same term after a far from innocuous content has been transferred onto it - form parts of a structure the originating linkages of which are given by the lines of the crystal. In proposing such a formulation for the problem, Lacan indicates that it is not as a metaphor that mathematics enters into the structure of the unconscious, but rather as an instrument of research, following and articulating pathways that stretch deep into the human soul.

The calming effect of the father function, once this father has himself shown that he can recognise and assume castration, allows Little Hans to cry less because of his horse. The structures that bear this function of intervention on the part of the father are not initially organised around a transference. However, there is a transference present within this material - in April 1906, for Hans's third birthday, Freud gave him a present: a rocking horse.

Teaching Transference

BIBLIOGRAPHICAL ADDENDUM:

Freud's arguments as to the structural priority of phobia, and its relation to the network of threads of interpretation are to be found in:

Freud, Sigmund: The Interpretation of Dreams (1900) in The Standard Edition of the Works of Sigmund Freud, Volumes IV, V, 1953.

Freud, Sigmund: 'Analysis of a Phobia in a Five-Year-Old Boy', 1909, in The Standard Edition of the Works of Sigmund Freud, Volume X, London, 1955.

Freud, Sigmund: 'The Question of Lay-Analysis: Conversations with an Impartial Person', 1926-7, in The Standard Edition of the Works of Sigmund Freud, Volume XX, London, 1959.

Herbert Graf's autobiographical reflections are contained in:

Graf, Herbert (Interview with Francis Rizzo): 'Memoirs of an Invisible Man', Parts I - IV, in Opera News, Vol. 36, Nos 11 - 14, Febuary 1972.

Herbert Graf's interpretations of the nature of art, and his own description of the projects that he initiated in his attempts to reorganise it, are to be found in:

Graf, Herbert: The Opera, and its Future in America, New York, 1941.

Graf, Herbert: Opera for the People, Minneapolis, 1951.

Graf, Herbert: Producing Opera for America, Zurich/New York, 1961.

Max Graf's relation to Freud, and the late formulations he gave to problems of philosophy and art are to be found in:

Graf, Max: 'Reminiscences of Professor Sigmund Freud', in The Psychoanalytic Quarterly, Vol. 11, No. 4, 1942.

Graf, Max: Jede Stunde War Erfüllt, Vienna-Frankfurt, 1957.

The Structural Problem in Phobia

For the theory of symbolism, and of the structures underlying object relations, see:

Jones, Ernest: 'The Theory of Symbolism', (1916), in Papers on Psycho-Analysis, 5th Edition, London, 1948.

Lacan, Jacques: 'A La Mémoire d'Ernest Jones: Sur sa Théorie du Symbolisme', in La Psychanalyse, Vol. 5, 1960; reprinted, with an appendix, in Ecrits, Paris, 1966.

Lacan, Jacques: Le Séminaire, Livre IV: La Relation d'Objet, 1956-1957, Paris, 1994.

Levi-Strauss, Claude: 'The Structural Study of Myth', in Myth, A Symposium: The Journal of American Folklore (Special Issue), Vol. 78, October - December 1955. This article is reprinted, in a variant form, as Chapter XI: 'La Structure des Mythes' in Anthropologie Structurale, Paris 1958, and translated from this revised form in Structural Anthropology, NewYork, 1963.

Imagos and the Problem of the Imaginary
Martin Stanton

Are unconscious structurings accessible to interpretation? Such a question may seem naive, given that much psychoanalytic work trades on the assumption that unconscious structurings are readily accessible to the analyst, hence can also be transmitted to the analysand. At the end of the session, or indeed the analysis, the analyst and analysand can point to material that was once unconscious, but through interpretation was made conscious. Even the unconscious structurings of the analytical session itself are standardly assumed to be transparent to interpretation: analysts talk of interpreting 'in' the transference, or 'in' the countertransference (the analyst's transference), implying that analyst's or analysand's place in the dialogue, as well as their specific communications, may be unconsciously structured, but that such structuring is nonetheless open to interpretation. In this way, interpreting in the transference means informing the analysand that he or she is not addressing the analyst but his or her mother or father or sibling; and interpreting in the countertransference means informing the analysand of the unconscious processes triggered off in the analyst by the analysand's communications.

Of course, the latter is extremely problematic, and leads to a second order of related questions: to what extent is the countertransference accessible to interpretation? Who then could or should interpret the countertransference? The analysand? The analyst's supervisor? Again, in this second order of questions, analysts standardly assume the priority and self-evidence of their interpretation as opposed to the analysand's supposed 'unconsciousness'. Hence the current (largely unquestioned) merging of questions of countertransference with the issue of projective identification (that is, the process by which the analysand projects into the analyst positive or negative transference feelings deriving from elsewhere but identified with the analyst): for example, if the analyst feels suddenly and inexplicably angry in a session, they will interpret it as the analysand's projective identification of bad feelings into them; the bad feelings are then conveniently disassociated from the specific unconscious dynamic of the analyst's (counter)transference.

One of Lacan's many great clinical achievements was to challenge the whole notion of the transparency of unconscious processes to interpretation, and indeed he went a considerable way in discrediting the false pervasive logic that accompanies such a position. I use the term 'clinical' here with specific intent, as many of Lacan's critics have tried to minimise the impact of his problematization of the unconscious structuring of interpretation. They claim that it is purely 'theoretical', by which they hope to separate theory from the interpretation of the 'reality' of the unconscious. For Lacan, and post-Lacanian analysts, there is no theory-less clinic, or 'clinical observation' of 'real' psychic process, including unconscious psychic process. There is no insulation of observation or theorisation from unconscious process. The desire to be an analyst (who is supposed to know) or the desire of the analysand to know (what it is supposed is known) not only rest on the logic of those suppositions, but also themselves articulate unconscious process. In short, there is no ultimate capture of unconscious process in 'real' knowledge based on clinical observation.

There is also no ultimate interpretative decoding of the unconscious structures that place analyst and analysand in a position to communicate with each other, so that 'transference' and 'countertransference' are given real form, like the silver scratched from a card to reveal familiar figures. On the contrary, the unconscious is traced out in the failures and gaps in de-coding, knowledge, and observation; transference and countertransference emerge when interpretation fails, and the analysis stalls.[1] The very point of interpretation, then, in analysis, is not to cement analyst or analysand in a fixed or 'secure' relation to the 'reality' of the unconscious, but precisely to subvert the pretension of the security of that 'reality' (or 'knowledge of 'reality ''), and indeed allow the symptom its unconscious root back : 'To liberate the word of the subject, we introduce him to the language of his desire, that is, to the first language in which, beyond what he says to us, he already speaks to us without knowing, and he speaks to us first and foremost in the symbols of the symptom'.[2]

---

[1] Lacan, J (1992), Le Transfert. Le Seminaire livre 8, Seuil, Paris.
[2] Lacan, J (1966), Ecrits, Seuil, Paris, p. 293.

Teaching Transference

Lacan's famous dictum 'The unconscious is structured as a language' has been subjected to many elaborations, many of them inaccurate. What has become clear, however, is that Lacan's notion of a 'first' language of the unconscious, namely desire, and a 'second' language in which we 'know' and communicate, is more complex than it first may have appeared (in glosses of the subject by Wilden, for example). [3] First of all, it is tied up with a developmental model in which the child's acquisition of language is seen as foundational to representation in general. In acquiring language, the child 'enters the Symbolic', which in turn permits a distinction with the 'first language' of the unconscious, as well as with a pre-linguistic Imaginary register of psychic life. Lacan's main, but not exclusive, paradigm for this was the 'mirror stage', which he elaborated in different ways, first in the 1930s,[4] then later between 1946 and 1949.[5] The mirror stage was originally conceived as a central foundational complex, which was developmentally linked to the prior 'weaning complex' (complexe du sevrage[6]) and the later Oedipus complex. In the mirror stage, the infant not only acquired a subject position in language through 'mirroring' and thus misrecognizing the image of the other, but also in the same process constructed a unified body image from the fragmentary and non-articulated body sites engaged in the process of weaning, notably surrounding the mother's breasts and inner body. Later, beginning with the 1955 paper 'The Freudian Thing', Lacan increasingly stressed the structural (as opposed to linear developmental) nature of the mirror stage, and moreover stressed the incomplete and aggressive dynamic of the mirror identification with the other:

> '...the precipitated identification of the 'I' with the other in the subject has the effect that this repartition never consti-

---

[3] Wilden, A (1965), The Language of the Self, Johns Hopkins, Baltimore.
[4] Lacan, J (1984), Les complexes familiaux dans la formation de l'individu, Navarin, Paris.
[5] Lacan, J, Ecrits, pp. 93-193.
[6] 'Sevrage' in French also implies 'cutting', as in 'cutting the umbilical cord', and 'separation' in the sense of 'cutting off' relations, which gives harsher connotations than the English term 'weaning'.

Imagos and the Problem of the Imaginary

tutes even a kinetic harmony, but is instituted on the permanent 'you or I' basis of a war...'[7]

Lacan clearly and consistently wished to stress the tension between the uncertain and aggressive negotiations of the mirror stage - or the 'fort/da' dynamic in which the infant established a secondary and incomplete mastery over objects through language [8] - and the fixed correlativity between the mirror stage and the Oedipus complex, installed ostensibly through the privilege of the phallus and the paternal metaphor in gaining access to the Symbolic register. Nonetheless, the balance between the uncertain and destabilising presence of the pre-Symbolic 'other' (negotiated through the fort/da), and the 'name of the Father' which held up the Symbolic register, remained significantly untheorised. One reason for this was Lacan's obvious doubts about the origin of paternal and parental inscription in the pre-symbolic or Imaginary; doubts first of all about the original derivation of infantile aggression, and the degree to which this may be parentally pre-inscribed; secondly, doubts about the special temporality of the mirror stage, notably whether the Imaginary register could only be established as such after the entry into the Symbolic, hence the special Lacanian reading in this context of 'afterwardsness' (Nachträglichkeit].[9]

These doubts and tensions are particularly evident in Lacan's early account of imagos, which he defines as primary psychic structures that enable the articulation of Imaginary elements in the Symbolic. Imagos both fix the primal identification of 'I' with the other, and hold the foundational tensions of misrecognition and aggression generated within the fort-da dynamic. Imagos therefore stabilise the primary identifications that found the subject, and establish an initial spatio-temporal discursivity (or 'causality' in early Lacanian terminology) for subjectivity. The linking or unlinking (liaison/deliason) between primary identifications in the fort/da dynamic are balanced out in imagos - which thus appear as fixed

---

[7] Lacan, J, Ecrits, p. 428

[8] Again it should be noted here that Lacan only later introduced the 'fort/da' dynamic (using Freud's exposition of the little Ernst's cotton reel game in Beyond the Pleasure Principle) to cast light on this aspect of the mirror stage ('The Function and Field of Speech and Language in Psychoanalysis', 1953, in Lacan, J, Ecrits, p. 103).

[9] (Lacan, 'Aggressivity in Psychoanalysis', [1948], in Lacan, J, Ecrits; Lacan, 'Function and Field... ', p 48.

'resolutions' or 'metamorphoses' in the subject's developing causal mastery of its identificatory space. Entry into the discursive world, then, depends not only on the illusion of psychic self-transparency (identification), but also on fixed, linked, and bound forms (imagos) which frame the fort/da dynamic in directive psychic causality (subjectivity):

' psychic causality itself [involves] identification, which is an irreducible phenomenon, and the imago, which is the definable form in the imaginary spatio-temporal complex whose function is to realise the resolving identification of a psychic phase, in other words, a metamorphosis of the relations of the individual with his/her similar other (semblable) '.[10]

Imagos therefore are central both to psychological enquiry - they have literally '...revolutionised psychology...', and even become '...the sole and proper object of psychology...'[11] - and foundational to the primary logic of subjectivity and discursivity. Within this paradigm, residual problems remain of explaining the innate developmental direction of discursivity itself - or the 'growth' of the human subject - and of accounting for the stabilising, 'fixative' and directive capacity of the imago, which supposedly must relate to some innate psychic logic (or 'auto-symbolic function', to use the contemporary psychoanalytic term [12]) . How could the imago as primary psychic form prescribe the form and function of the Symbolic register, at the same time as holding access to the pre-verbal, pre-subjective Imaginary ? Did the imago deaden the aggressivity of the fort/da dynamic through an auto-symbolic psychic function ? Furthermore, did the imago 'fix' the fort/da dynamic through the instalment of fantasy, that is, a non-Real (non-relational) closed scene in which the living-being-ontological-experienced-present

---

[10] Lacan, 'Proposals on Psychic Causality', Ecrits, p. 188.

[11] Lacan, J, Ecrits, p. 188.

[12] The 'autosymbolic function' was a term introduced by Herbert Silberer to account for the psyche's capacity to represent its own functions (Silberer, H. (1970), Problems of Mysticism and its Symbolism, Weiser, New York). Freud significantly introduces this term into his 'Considerations of Representability' in the Interpretation of Dreams (SE, V, p. 344 ff.), to discuss the 'translation' problems between abstractions and the primary pictorial language of dreams.

Imagos and the Problem of the Imaginary

(Erlebnis or Dasein in the phenomenological-existentialist tradition [13]) was shut down into an inner object-related world [14] ?

Lacan's attempts to answer these questions involved an extended critical engagement with Melanie Klein's work on the form and function of the imago. In May 1948, when he presented a 'theoretical report' on the subject to the 11th Congress of French-Speaking Psychoanalysts, he clearly felt a profound sense of common purpose with the Kleinian approach:

> 'Through her we know the function of the imaginary primordial enclosure formed by the imago of the mother's body; through her we have the cartography, drawn by the children's own hands, of the mother's internal empire, the historical atlas of the intestinal divisions in which the imagos of the father and brothers (real or virtual), in which the

---

[13]. Mikkel Borch-Jacobsen wrongly assumes that the Lacanian engagement with the imago relates primarily to the specular origin and formation of the Real, as articulated through particular readings of Hegel, Heidegger, and Sartre (in contrast to an empiricist dependence on Bühler, Caillois, and Wallon). It is strange—or perhaps 'uncanny'—that he ignores the clinical presence/experience (Dasein/Erlebnis) of Lacan's engagement with the concept of the imago, namely the fraught question of how to negotiate the 'fixity'—or non-narratability and non-translatability—of symptoms, especially in clinical work with repetition-constraints (Zwangsneurosen), obsessions, and phobias. In this context, the 'fixity' of the imago—its various static, timeless, monumental, statuesque, architectural, and archetypal associations appealed to by Borch-Jacobsen—cannot possibly relate to a 'Reality of true ideal forms' (Borch-Jacobsen, M (1991), Lacan: the absolute master, Stanford University Press, Stanford, California, p. 63), but to a Real marked out by the resistance of a given symptom to any interpretative process whatsoever.

[14] Laplanche raises similar questions with regard to the status of 'fantasy' in psychoanalysis:

'what is already imposed with the notion of fantasy (fantasme), if one does not take it in the Sartrean phenomenal sense of the imaginal, but as a scenario which has no aim (or no more aim) other than itself, and which finds its satisfaction in itself. It is certainly the dream which provides the most suggestive analogon of these characteristics: closure on itself, as much in the closure of its story (recit) as in the fulfilment of desire in a purely immanent way. The imago, a term deriving from Jung, rightly adopted by psychoanalysis, represents the 'object' side in respect to the 'relation' side in the fantasy. Certainly to qualify this object, to speak of 'castrating father' or 'good breast' implies that these imagos are caught in the fantasies; but they represent the most static aspect of it; perhaps also the most abyssal aspect of it, to the extent that, in the unconscious, the deepest is the level at which the relation resolves itself in its elements.' (Laplanche, J. (1987), Problematiques 5, Le Baquet: Transcendance du transfert, PUF, Paris, p. 263)

Teaching Transference

voracious aggression of the subject himself, dispute the deleterious dominance over her sacred regions'[15].

Nonetheless, Lacan is also clearly troubled by the direct personification (of mothers, fathers, and brothers) in the Kleinian imagos, which are installed problematically in a 'good' or 'bad' way through identification with gratification or lack of gratification. In the Kleinian imago, he perceives

> '...the persistence in the subject of this shadow of the bad internal objects, linked with some accidental association (to use a term that we should accept in the organic sense that it assumes in our experience, as opposed to the abstract sense that it retains in Humean ideology). Hence we can understand by what structural means the re-evocation of certain imaginary personae, the reproduction of certain situational inferiorities may disconcert in the most strictly predictable way the adult's voluntary functions; namely, their fragmenting effect on the imago of the original identification'.[16]

For Lacan, crucial here are the 'disconcerting' effects of the feedback of subsequent imagos on the original imago which installs the subject through misrecognition. The Kleinian personification of the imagos, and its fixation of them around the 'good' and 'bad' identifications with parental bodies and figures, implies a single developmental plane leading through a series of set imagos towards a predetermined psychic self-regulatory agency, the super-ego. For Klein, the functional role of imagos remains simple and unproblematic:

> '...these figures [imagos] represent intermediate stages between the terrible menacing super-ego, which is totally divorced from reality and the identifications which approximate more closely to reality. These intermediate figures, whose gradual evolution into the maternal and paternal helpers (who are nearer again to reality) may constantly be observed in play analyses, and seem very instructive for our knowledge of the formation of the super-ego.'[17]

---

[15] Lacan, J, Ecrits, p. 20.
[16] Lacan, J, Ecrits, p. 21.
[17] Klein, M. (1975), Love, Guilt, and Reparation, Hogarth, London, p.203).

Imagos and the Problem of the Imaginary

Lacan's principal objection to this is the implicit syncretism between psychic agencies (notably the ego and the super-ego) and a Real that is pre-constructed around fixed parental figures. Imagos for Lacan articulate pre-subjective (pre-ego) drives in the Imaginary, so structurally must serve to subvert and disrupt the unitary forces of subjectivity accessed through the Symbolic. For Lacan, then, imagos are essentially structured as 'the elective vectors of aggressive intentions' (Lacan, 1977, p.10), so any perceived developmental 'purpose' in them must be subversive or regressive. In contrast to Klein, he proposes therefore that the primary imagos are those of the fragmented body:

> 'The imagos of the fragmented body articulate the death-drive: these are the imagos of castration, mutilation, dismemberment, dislocation, evisceration, devouring, and bursting open of the body.'[18]

Following these imagos, the subject's subsequent construction of a unified body-image negates (through misrecognition) this fragmentation. The subject's re-mapping of a unified body image, and its subsequent sense of body agency, are therefore constantly threatened by the original 'vectors of aggressive intention'. This is best illustrated by play between children of about eight months, particularly '...those gestures of fictitious actions by which a subject reconducts the imperfect effort of the other's gesture by confusing their distinct application, those synchronies of spectacular captation that are all the more remarkable in that they precede the complete co-ordination of the motor apparatuses that they bring into play.'[19]

The Lacanian concept of the imago was therefore structurally different from the Kleinian concept. First and foremost, Lacan maintained that imagos subverted subjectivity rather than reinforced it (as in the Kleinian parental and combined parental imagos). For Lacan, the subversion of the imago was visible in its effects, which were essentially fragmentary or 'cut-up' (morcele). Imagos were fragmentary because they captured and fixed an element of Imaginary destructive drive in the Symbolic; they articulated absence, loss, and damage to subjectivity, notably through

---

[18] Lacan, J, Ecrits, p. 11.
[19] Lacan, J, Ecrits, p. 18.

castration, mutilation, dismemberment, dislocation, evisceration, devouring, and bursting open of the body (in the imagos of the fragmented body). Crucial for Lacan here was the intrusion of such imagos in the subjective perception of the body: such imagos not only provoked the 'narcissistic fear of damage to one's own body', which Lacan viewed as 'psychologically prior to the fear of death', but also disrupted the functional unity of the body, notably visible in somatoform and eating disorders [20].

It is particularly significant here that Lacan regarded the body as the prime site of the disruptive inscription of the imago, and that the bodily inscription itself remained Imaginary - that is, it was fixed but unprocessed symbolically. There is no question at this point of incorporating the imago in the symbolic. Indeed, for Lacan, this constitutes Klein's fundamental error:

> ' So what did Melanie Klein actually do? - nothing other than to bring in verbalisation. She symbolised an effective relationship, that of one named being with another. She plastered on the symbolisation of the Oedipal myth, to give it its real name'.[21]

Alternatively, Lacan could not abandon the clear Oedipal configurations of his imagos of the fragmented body, notably of the imago of castration and its extension in the Symbolic through the paternal metaphor (which curiously resonates here with Klein's 'one named being with another' cited above).

In contrast to Klein, the Lacanian imago remains fundamentally sensory, and this element of it resists any associative and interpretative integration in the Symbolic. In fact, this view strictly follows Freud's 'considerations of representability'. For Freud, verbal narratives are either secondary or disarticulated from pictorial ones, so

---

[20] Lacan, J, Ecrits, p. 28. Adrian Stokes applied similar notions to the aesthetic perception of the body:
'We cannot discover in our own bodies the nude entirely. Narcissistic sensitivity obscures contemplation. Sex-organs often continue to be viewed as part-objects unintegrated with the tenor of the body ... the totality of the nude may rarely have shone, yet the potential power will have made itself deeply felt. I propose that the respect thus founded for the general body is the seal upon our respect for other human beings as such ...' (Stokes, A (1978), The Critical Writings of Adrian Stokes, Thames & Hudson, London, p. 304.)
[21] Lacan, J (1988), The Technical Writings of Freud. The Seminar Book 1, trans. J. Forrester & S. Tomaselli, Cambridge University Press, Cambridge, p. 85)

Imagos and the Problem of the Imaginary

'translations' between the two residually fail to integrate the two orders, leaving an 'excess' - an untranslated, un-processed, fixed element that remains unconscious.[22] The problem with this view is precisely the status of the primal connection between the Imaginary and the Symbolic. At this stage, Lacan suggests a priority of sensory inscription, or auditory, visual, olfactory and neuro-affective inscriptions, which elude capture in either the Imaginary or the Symbolic, but connect up to both orders 'negatively' by their resistance to conscious process (as 'unconscious') and their residual indication of absence (as fragmentation or absence of wholeness). In this way, the imagos of the fragmented body articulate sensory inscriptions on or in the body which both underpin verbal narratives and threaten their connection to and articulation of the Imaginary. In this scenario, the Imaginary order is constructed retrospectively (Nachträglichkeit) in the Mirror Stage around a primal identification whose imago provokes both entry into the Symbolic world, and the residual failure of the Symbolic to capture and cohere its primary sensory inscription.

The essential function of the imago in Lacanian analysis then is to articulate the complex connections between the Symbolic and the Imaginary in residual specific sensory inscriptions. These complex connections themselves articulate the Real - or that which pre-structures the configuration of the Imaginary and the Symbolic in the specific subjective process. The projective, essentially fragile, and self-subverting status of this Real, explains both the abstraction and the transformative nature of the imagos (as 'elective vectors of aggressive intentions'). Moreover, this abstraction and transformation is not articulated cognitively by the imago, but by its specific residual sensory component. The abstraction does not represent a theory or theoretical process but the articulation of primary unconscious sensory inscriptions. A more accurate analogy here is with abstract expressionism in art - particularly in the work of Pollock, Gorky, Rothko, and Motherwell.[23]

---

[22] Freud, S. (1953), The Standard Edition of the Complete Psychological Works of Sigmund Freud, Hogarth, London, p. 340.
[23] Stanton, M (1993), 'Painting the Nightmare: Jackson Pollock's Psychoanalytic Drawings', Modern Painters, **6**, 4; (1994), 'L'apres-coup et les problemes de figuration a l'origine du symptome', Colloque international de psychanalyse: actes du colloque de Montreal 1992 , ed. Jacques Andre, PUF, Paris.

Teaching Transference

The imago did not disappear then in Lacan's work after the 1953 'linguistic breakthrough' - any more than the signifier disappeared in the 1970 'matheme-borromean knot breakthrough'. Rather, the concern for conditions of representability of the pre-subjective were transformed through different formalisations. Indeed, it was one of Lacan's favourite strategies to structure possible re-workings, re-translations, and re-visitations to his texts (exemplified prominently in the Ecrits, with their enigmatic prefaces, and in the Seminar project, which, in retrospect, seemed specially designed to bring out its 'errata'.[24] Curiously, Lacan seemingly moved on from the concept of the imago at precisely the same time he declared it essential to all future psychoanalytic work with psychosis. On the one hand, he proclaimed that the 'essential trait' of the imago indicated '...generic resemblances, which imply a certain primitive recognition' - which meant that they offered a unique access to 'types' of mental disorder, and to the generational transmission of disorders.[25] On the other hand, he suggested that further work with imagos demanded culturally specific perceptual skills, like the desert hunter looking for 'imperceptible traces', or 'listening for the steps of a gazelle on the rocks' - in short, special skills derived from psychoanalytic work with major 'generic types' of mental dis order like psychosis, borderline, and bipolar disorders (notably involving hallucinations).[26]

---

[24] ELP (Ecole Lacanienne de Psychanalyse) (1991), Le transfert dans tous ses errata, EPEL, Paris.
[25] Lacan, J, Ecrits, p.181.
[26] Lacan, J, Ecrits, p. 193.

Letters and Symptoms: Lacan and literature
Luke Thurston

I

The tangled *Ubersetzung* - transfer, coitus, translation - between literature and psychoanalysis begins with a letter; written by Freud to Fliess on October 15th 1897 -

> ' ... Fleetingly the thought passed through my head that the same thing [i.e. the Oedipus complex, whose discovery he has just announced] might be at the bottom of Hamlet as well. I am not thinking of Shakespeare's conscious intention, but believe, rather, that a real event stimulated the poet to his representation, in that his unconscious understood the unconscious of his hero'.[1]

With this notion of literature as 'pathography' - somehow a textual 'equivalent' to the psychical suffering shown in the speech of his patients - Freud opened up the field of 'applied' psychoanalysis, which would be explored by later authors across a wide range of aesthetic questions, in 'psychobiography' and so on. The Freudian discovery seemed to find in art its own mirror-image, strangely distorted : a domain where 'the same thing' (as had first been given rational articulation by psychoanalysis) emerged in a protean array of quasi-symptomatic forms. If, on the one hand, the literary text - as a representational network strewn with conflicts, desires, compromises - 'resembled' the symptoms of neurotic illness, at the same time the interpretive labour of the analyst, seeking to 'decipher' the rebus-like conundrums of the analysand's desire, itself came to resemble an act of reading, the critical scanning of meaning in the intricate webs of a text.

Jacques Lacan's tongue-in-cheek 'advice to a young psychoanalyst' in 1953 - 'Do cross-words' - is thus part of a Freudian tradition, the conception of analysis as an 'hermeneutics', an elaborate

---

[1] The Complete Letters of Sigmund Freud to Wilhelm Fliess, translated and edited by J M Masson (Bellknap:Harvard, 1985), p. 272.

kind of riddle-solving.² Lacan's reading of Hamlet (in the 1958-9 seminar, *Désir et son Interprétation*) nevertheless sought to rescue the play from 'the psychoanalytic wisdom of Polonius' - from what had already become 'Freudian' clichés (of the kind found, say, in Ernest Jones' Hamlet and Oedipus (1949)) - by refiguring the question of 'the unconscious' and the text in the terminology of structuralism. Hamlet is 'always at the hour of the Other', dependent on the signifier and its inscription of the Law.³ In one sense, however, this 'de-psychologized' structuralist Hamlet remains resolutely Freudian. By isolating as the essential moment of the play 'the subject's appointment with the hour of his destruction', Lacan admits he has done nothing but indicate something which, like the Oedipus complex for Freud, 'is meaningful in the destiny of every individual.'⁴ If for Freud Shakespeare's text is haunted by the presence of its author, who comes complete with various pieces of unconscious baggage, for Lacan in 1959 the play still (re)presents the subject. The Freudian symptom, whether or not it appears 'in' a text, is always read as the trace of the subject, a subject appended to the (unconscious) text in a relation of sheer transcendence. Perhaps a glimpse of the extent to which Lacan later sought to break free from the Freudian subject, and the 'aesthetics' it entailed, is given by the statement he made in 1976:

> 'To explain art with the unconscious seems to me to be highly suspect; but it is what analysts do. It seems to me more serious to explain art with the symptom.'⁵

II

> 'I am not attempting to produce a philosophy of art. I am too busy with the consequences of my practice, which is absolutely punctiform - it is only at a limited number of

---

² 'Fonction et champ de la parole et du langage en psychanalyse', in Écrits (Paris:du Seuil, 1966), p. 266; my translation.
³ 'Desire and the Interpretation of Desire in Hamlet', in Literature and Psychoanalysis; the Question of Reading: Otherwise, ed. Shoshana Felman (London;Johns Hopkins, 1982), p. 25.
⁴ (ibid.).
⁵ Scilicet 6/7, 1975, p. 36.

specific points that it touches on the domain of art.' Jacques Lacan[6]

Why should symptom be the key to the Lacanian engagement with literature? To trace the history of the term in Lacan's thought is to encounter different moments in a shifting conceptualisation of the relation between the subject and language in psychoanalysis - of the subject's place in, determination by signification. If Lacan once remarked dismissively that 'literature' was a mere academic convention, this was because the letter played too important a role in his conception of human existence merely to be confined to the backwaters of 'applied psychoanalysis'.[7] Rather than seeking to assume the false position of a metalanguage, capable of decoding artistic 'pathography', psychoanalysis should, Lacan believed, seek in literature the opportunity to learn more about *l'instance de la lettre*.

A certain radical ambiguity is inherent to the notion of symptom in psychoanalysis. On the one hand, as product of the unconscious, the symptom remains in essence opaque, 'meaningless': like Dora's repetitive cough, it is fuelled by the blind compulsion of the drive, irreducible to the ordered syntax of communication. And yet Freud found that this inert trace was nevertheless enmeshed in signification, that it was always a kind of 'message', caught up in and multiply 'overdetermined' by, interconnecting and conflictual patterns of thought. Lacan's earlier work found this ambiguity perfectly captured in the terms of structural linguistics:

> 'The symptom is here the signifier of a signified repressed from the subject's consciousness. A symbol written on the sands of the flesh, on the veil of Maia, it forms part of language in its semantic ambiguity ... '[8]

With the symptom conceived as signifier, the work of the analyst became *déchiffrage* ('deciphering'), the attempt to unravel the 'cryptography' caused by repression and psychical conflict, to render the analysand's desire legible. In one sense, the 'optimism' of this structuralist moment - its 'Enlightenment' goal of rational self-presentation beyond any contingent distortion or falsification - per-

---

[6] Scilicet 6/7, 1975, p. 21.
[7] See Lacan's seminar at Yale University in 1975: 'literature ... is what can be found in manuals' (Scilicet 6/7, 1975), p. 33.
[8] Écrits, p. 280-1.

sists throughout Lacan's career: as late as 1973, he is still ascribing to Freud 'un déchiffrage de dit-mension signifiante pure'.⁹ From as early as the publication of the *Écrits*, however, Lacan adds to this picture a note which hints that the emergence of analytic 'truth' involves more than simply solving a cross-word puzzle:

> 'Unlike the sign - smoke never without fire, the fire it indicates, calling eventually for it to be extinguished - the symptom can only be interpreted in the order of the signifier. The signifier only has meaning in relation to another signifier. It is in this articulation that the truth of the symptom dwells. The symptom has kept a blur to represent [un flou de représenter] the irruption of truth. It actually is truth, is made of the same stuff as it - if as materialists we posit truth as that which sets up the signifying chain.'¹⁰

The 'truth of the symptom' is on the one hand a function of its place in the differential weave of signification; but at the same time, truth is 'represented' in or by some kind of symptomatic 'blur', which 'sets up' (*instaure*) the entire signifying network. Lacan sums up this ambiguous position of the symptom - both embedded in language and somehow transcending it, opaque to it - with his remark in *Télévision*: although the symptom 'consists' in a 'knot of signifiers' - these are 'not of *sens* ('meaning') but of *jouis-sens*' ('enjoyment-meaning', punning on *jouissance*).¹¹

'How do *jouissance* and *sens* combine in the writing of the symptom *(l'écriture du symptôme)*?' Jacques-Alain Miller claims that the question 'runs from end to end through [Lacan's] teaching'.¹² The famous Lacanian formula of the 'unconscious structured like a language' may perhaps, in its reliance on the Saussurean 'signifier', have risked effacing a crucial feature of language: the radically different positions of the subject in speech and writing. Miller recalls, however, that as early as the mid-1950s Lacan had pinpointed precisely this kind of difference around the notion of symptom. If, Lacan had argued in 'La Psychanalyse et son enseignement' (1957), in psychoanalysis the transferential space

---

⁹ 'The decipherment of the pure signifying aspect of speech'; Télévision (du Seuil, 1973), p.20. *Dit-mension* is a favourite pun of Lacan in the 1970s.
¹⁰ 'Du sujet enfin en question' (1966), in *Écrits*, pp. 234-5; my translation.
¹¹ Télévision, p. 22.
¹² 'Préface', Joyce Avec Lacan (Paris:Navarin, 1987), ed. Jacques Aubert; p. 11.

Letters and Symptoms

opened by the analysand's speech allowed the symptom to be 'read', producing certain effects of meaning, the symptom 'in itself' remained 'inscribed in a writing process', an enciphered trace of 'autistic' *jouissance*.[13] Thus, in the 'Seminar on the Purloined Letter', Lacan stresses - with a quotation from Joyce: a letter, a litter - the objectal quality of the sign, the 'remnant' beyond its signifying message. This 'deposit', as an embodiment of a 'real' defined as the evacuation of meaning, became the central interest of the late seminars. Lacan turned to Joyce's texts again in 1975; as Miller puts it, this time his aim was

> 'to start out from writing in order to put in question psychoanalysis in the field of language'.[14]

III

> 'I've put in so many enigmas and puzzles that it will keep the professors busy for centuries arguing over what I meant; and that's the only way of ensuring one's immortality.'
>
> James Joyce[15]

At one point in *Le Sinthome*, the 'Joycean' seminar of 1975-6, Lacan makes clear that it is certainly not his intention to 'analyse' Joyce. 'A certain Chechner', he remarks,

> has wished to analyse *Ulysses*. The impression this gives is absolutely terrifying; it truly gives one the idea that the novelist's imagination - the imagination which reigns over *Ulysses* - is to be chucked in the dustbin'.[16]

By a certain irony, it was precisely a view of the texts as Joycean 'litter' - the 'indecipherable' writing of jouis-sens - that Lacan adopted, in order to avoid lapsing into any 'application' of psychoanalytic theory. The split between signifier and letter which sepa-

---

[13] Lacan, Écrits, pp. 444-5.
[14] Joyce Avec Lacan.
[15] Richard Ellman, *James Joyce* (Oxford, 1982), p. 521.
[16] *Le Sinthome*, 13/01/76, Ornicar? 1976; my translation.

rated 'analytic' effects, together with the subject they 'supposed' (in transference) from the objectal 'stuff' of language, was elaborated into another, related theoretical split: between symptom - now defined as *le façon dont chacun jouit de l'inconscient*, the particularity of unconscious *jouissance* - and symbol. This last division amounted, in the end, to nothing less than a reconceptualisation of the 'symbolic'; that Lacan never 'finished' this re-thinking of the relations between language and the subject was perhaps not simply an accident of time.

Joyce's writing, in its singular 'disarticulation' of language, manifests for Lacan the 'pure' form of the symptom. This 'real' of the symptom is given a new name, *sinthome*: no longer a signifier 'representing the subject for another signifier', it is now conceived as a writing which in some way 'allows [the subject] to live'.

How can this transformation of the term 'symptom' be understood? The Freudian notion of analysis as 'dissolution' of symptoms, in which the 'riddle' of the analysand's desire would be definitively solved, given an 'answer' by the analyst, relied on a specific, 'Enlightenment' notion of the sign: as pharmaceutical, redemptive or liberating.[17] Lacan's early work, with its conception of analysis as *déchiffrage*, the symbolic mastery or 'abolition' of symptomatic 'riddles', was in direct continuity with this 'modern' Freudian ambition, to use language to dispel the mists of deceit or pathology. For Lacan to restate the aim of analysis as he did on 13th January 1976 - 'we teach the analysand to splice together his symptom and the parasitic real of *jouissance*' - thus indicates a veritable 'revolution' in his account of the subject.[18] By the mid-1970s, the symbolic is no longer accorded the primacy it had enjoyed at the time of 'high' structuralism, when it held the supreme position in the subject, as its 'true' representation. It has become, rather, a component of the Borromean knot - which had been drawn up in the seminar of 1974-5, RSI, as a new topology of the subject in which the three orders real, symbolic and imaginary are constitutively inter-linked. The place of the symptom, as it was situated in the topological elaborations of *Le Sinthome*, was precisely to main-

---

[17] Cf. Slavoj Zizek's comments on Lacan's Joyce and 'the triad realism-modernism-postmodernism' in The Indivisible Remainder: An Essay on Schelling and Related Matters (London:Verso, 1996), pp. 202, 233.

[18] *Le Sinthome*, 13/01/76.

Letters and Symptoms

tain the coherence of the knot RSI, to safeguard its 'borromean' structure (each order fully entwined with the other two). Rather than seeking to do away with the symptom, analysis now deployed it, put it to work as a crucial element in the operation of 'splicing' and suture.

Lacan's turn to the Borromean knot to theorise the structure of the subject completely recast the question of 'the letter' and its instance. The famous 'foreclosure of the name-of-the-father', in which the absence of a certain symbolic investment led to a psychotic 'return in the real', was now deemed only one of the ways that the knot could 'slip': 'radical foreclosure' corresponded to a more drastic 'un-knotting', where 'the real forecloses meaning' (*le sens*, conceived as the joint effect of the symbolic and the imaginary).[19] Joyce's writing was identified as a response, exemplified for Lacan in the youthful 'epiphanies', to just such topological unravelling: a singular *réparation sinthomatique* through which Joyce salvaged his coherence as a subject.

Cathérine Millot has explored this notion of re-knotting, by looking more closely at the Joycean 'epiphany'. Accepting Lacan's re-conception of foreclosure as a form of *dénouage*, she notes that

> ' ... the epiphanic experience corresponds to the first knot between the loops of the symbolic and the real, which causes the third loop, the imaginary, to drop away 'like a fruit shedding its tender and ripe skin'. Writing, however, is situated at the place of Joyce's ego - which, re-knotting a second time the symbolic and the real, includes in the second knot the imaginary left free in the first. Writing re-establishes the knot RSI.'[20]

If, in radical foreclosure, meaning is emptied out by *jouissance*, Joyce's *sinthomatique* writing responded with an 'overdetermination' of meaning, to produce, as Millot puts it, 'the coalescence of an excessive meaning with its evacuation'.[21] An epiphany, Joyce wrote in the early manuscript Stephen Hero, was 'a sudden spiritual manifestation, whether in the vulgarity of speech or of gesture or

---

[19] Le Sinthome, 11/05/76.
[20] Cathérine Millot, 'épiphanies', in Joyce Avec Lacan, p. 92; my translation.
[21] Millot, p. 91; my translation.

in a memorable phase of the mind itself'.[22] But it is the presence of the *body* which disrupts meaning in these short, fragmentary texts:

> Mrs Joyce - (crimson, trembling, appears at the parlour door) ... Jim!
> Joyce - (at the piano) ... Yes?
> Mrs Joyce - Do you know anything about the body? ... ... What ought I do? ... There's some matter coming away from the hole in Georgie's stomach ... Did you ever hear of that happening?
> Joyce - (surprised) ... I don't know ...
> Mrs Joyce - Ought I send for the doctor, do you think?
> Joyce - I don't know ... ... What hole?
> Mrs Joyce - (impatient) ... The hole we all have ... here (points)
> Joyce - (stands up)[23]

The 'hole we all have' is the invisible and traumatic 'centre' of the text, where the 'matter' (punning, like Hamlet, on mater)it puts forth disappears, like the umbilical vanishing-point of the Freudian dream. The epiphany dramatises itself as a failure of knowledge, the *insu que sait* in which its characters are trapped 'here', in this text.[24] The lack of meaning or signifying matter is counterbalanced, as Millot observes, by an excessive, 'tautological' sense-production: the double gesture towards the contingent stuff of the body (accentuated by the vivid effects of emotional expression and movement) and towards the linguistic 'substance' of the text ('this hole' ... 'here').

The traumatic *jouissance* which for Lacan threatened to unravel the subjective knot, causing the imaginary (and thus the possibility of *sens*) to 'come away' from the wounding collision of the symbolic

---

[22] Stephen Hero Ed. Theodore Spencer (London:Cape 1969), p. 211.

[23] 'Epiphany 19', March 1902; in Poems and Epiphanies, Ed. R Ellman & A.W.Li(New York:Viking, 1990)

[24] The year after Le Sinthome, 1976-7, Lacan gave his seminar a delirious pun as title: L'insu que sait de l'une-bévue s'aile à mourre. Its first phrase, punning on l'insuccès, 'failure', rephrased the Freudian unconscious as a paradoxical form of knowledge, 'the unknown that knows'.

Letters and Symptoms

and the real, is 'tied' by the writing-process back into a 'borromean' structure; a structure which is the subject.[25]

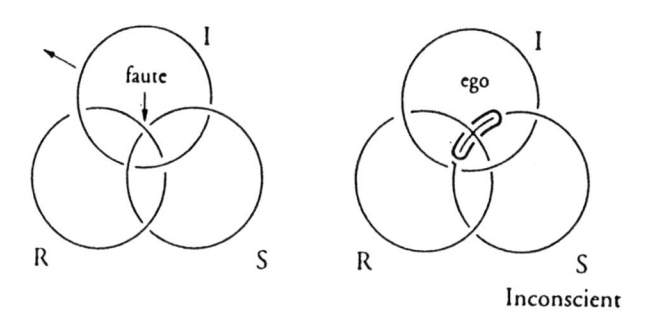

In one sense, this theory of the text as a *sinthomatique* 'response' to radical foreclosure dealt nicely with the hackneyed question of biographical speculation which usually arose in psychoanalytic accounts of art. If the origin of the text was the 'foreclosure' of meaning, the utter collapse of the subject, how could it offer the biographer any clues to a transcendent subjective 'depth', of the sort, say, that Freud had looked for in the paintings of Leonardo? For Lacan, Joyce's writing was a strategy of self-invention, an *autography*, in which the text itself stitched together its 'subject'. The subject was thus immanent to the *sinthome* - the author identical with his text (thus '*Joyce le symptôme*'). Lacan went so far as claiming that Joyce was *désabonné à l'inconscient*, 'had withdrawn his investment' from the unconscious: the *parlêtre* ('speaking-being', the term with which Lacan 'translated' the Freudian unconscious) was replaced by the *sinthome*, a 'writing-being'.[26] The texts bore witness to the irreducible *jouissance* of their 'primal scenes' - the epiphanic foreclosures of Joyce's infancy - rather than being simply caught up in, products of, the inter-subjective texture of the unconscious.

---

[25] This diagram is a slightly modified version of one given in an article by Pierre Skriabine, 'Clinique et Topologie' (1989), printed in Logique Lacanienne. The picture on the right, indicating the re-knotting with the sinthome, marked as S in this version, is marked 'ego' by Skriabine; in French this does not refer to le moi (the English 'ego'), but rather the 'I', as the minimal place of subjective agency.
[26] See Lacan's address to the 5th International James Joyce Symposium, 'Joyce le symptôme', in Joyce Avec Lacan, pp. 25-7.

133

Teaching Transference

Lacan's portrait of the artist as a *sinthome* is deliberately paradoxical. Joyce had notoriously refused a patron's offer of the financial support which would have allowed an analysis with Jung; he was not, as Lacan puts it, *mordu par l'analyse*, he 'didn't think much' of psychoanalysis. For Lacan, this refusal was an amusing 'confirmation' of the place of Joyce's work: *beyond analysis*. This 'beyond' offered the psychoanalyst a unique lesson in the *instance* of the letter and the unlikely possibilities of *suture* it afforded. The 'transference' between analysis and literature could thus entail, not the 'dissolution' of a literary symptom into the subject of psychoanalysis, but the production of a new kind of theoretical 'knot', as a question addressed to that very subject.

A Sound Idea
Rosemary Dunn

There was a sign on the door of the Chemistry laboratory at school: 'What in the world is not Chemistry?' I had passed that challenging question several times a day for some time and found it extremely provoking for, to me, the answer was obvious. As a teacher though, I knew I must choose my moment to act, so when there was nobody about one day I triumphantly wrote underneath: 'Music!' No-one removed the defaced notice - no-one further defaced it or added other comments, and there it remained, loaded with assumptions - a daily reminder of my cathartic reaction. To others, my act may appear insignificant, even pathetic, but to me it was an expression of my deeply-felt antagonism to the arrogance implicit in the question. My written reply expressed this antagonism perfectly, while at the same time, I was hoping to imply a moral superiority for music, by virtue of its inclusivity.

Music is everywhere - yet nowhere in particular. Music is sound - it is also silence. Its elements seem easily measurable, yet its mystique is impossible to quantify. We know that everything which moves creates a wave which has a potential to sound, and music, in its widest sense, is understood simply as elements of sound with culturally acquired organisational patterns and aesthetics. It has extremely detailed and complex specialisms, yet is so much more than a human creation - sounds being here long before we were. It is so all-embracing a phenomenon as to have the right to claim to be a universal fundament. Its importance as such can be appreciated within an historical perspective, but then it must first be divested of its culturally-specific accretions. Music has a place in myth, religion, language, art and science as both a conscious and unconscious element and affect; it is a unifying, not a separate metaphysical phenomenon. Perhaps that would seem sufficient to justify claiming an inclusivity for music, but there is a further related dimension to consider; music has a role as a containing space.

Many and varied are the discourses inspired by music as a result of its inclusivity, but I feel inevitably drawn towards an exploration of this particular role. A containing space can be large or small;

both a receptacle and a resource, protective and defensive; it can be filled or emptied, closed or opened, plundered or replenished - in fact it is a metaphor with virtually unlimited potential. I acknowledge that, since writing the word 'music' seemed to be so important a reaction to me, my conscious mind appeared at the mercy of the activated contents of this containing space. Am I therefore claiming for music, a space which is a metaphor for the unconscious itself? Given present restrictions, this question initiates an impossibly large area of enquiry, but in addressing the 'inevitability' of my interest in music's role as a containing space, I hope to render a significant contribution to the debate.

The adduction of psychoanalytic theory to the investigation of musical phenomena, is probably best within an hermeneutic of Critical Idealism; for the sensate, affective experience of sounds renders inadequate a purely scientific, cognitive approach. Psycho-biology and psycho-acoustics are fundamental to any enquiry into the measurable determinants of the creation, performance and appreciation of music; but there is a sense in which the abstract concept of music as a containing space in the mind, allows for all that is unmeasurable, all that is emotional affect in music - in fact, that which constitutes the mystique of music. This space should be the specific province of metapsychological investigation, as it has consistently proved to be resistant to empiricism, leaving us with a challenging cultural gap. Once the possibility is recognised that this containing space is in the unconscious mind, Psychoanalytic theory can be brought to bear upon the investigation.

My present investigative position can be best understood from an appreciation of the inspiration derived from my teaching career. Spanning over thirty years, this has involved me in training and conducting choirs, bands and orchestras; teaching theory, harmony and counterpoint, music analysis and the history of music; while at the same time enjoying playing viola in orchestras, encompassing the main orchestral and choral repertoire. The most formative moment for me though, came in the earliest weeks of my first teaching appointment, in a South London comprehensive school. There I came across twelve-year-old Carol, a self-taught pianist, rather tentatively improvising at the piano. As I was preparing the incidental music for a school production of Oliver Twist at the time, I asked her if she would like to compose some music for this. The result was a collection of short pieces which she memorised

A Sound Idea

and performed during the play. In those days, for a schoolgirl to compose her own music was considered so unusual that the Times Educational Supplement reported the achievement! Shortly afterwards, Carol moved away from the area, so I was unable to follow her progress, but here was 'a very ordinary child' turning her improvisations into small works of art. Significantly, I guessed that if she could do it, then so could most, given the tools to do it with, and thus began my exploration of musical creativity - not as a specialism confined to a few, but as a general accomplishment. Consequently, my expectation that pupils could compose, and that some would exhibit a particular preference for doing so, established reciprocal expectations in the pupils, and became the motivating force behind all my work.[1]

Any reasonably comprehensive system of music teaching will provide sufficient knowledge for a pupil to begin composing their own music. In addition, the persuasion of the teacher that composition can be a practical use and manifestation of consciously acquired knowledge, may well result in pupil compositions. But, by and large, the resulting compositions predicated upon this method alone are disappointing - they will be no more than a pastiche of a preferred, assimilated style. All too often these productions receive uncritical acclaim because they conform to common perceptions of what music is. If, on the other hand, the teacher is sensitive to the student's 'need to be heard', the process of encouraging the student to express this need can begin. Through the student's selection of musical ideas (manifest in particular arrangements of sounds) which are 'worked through' in the development of a composition, a unique, personal aesthetic is engendered. I maintain that it is the constituents of this personal aesthetic which exist in the containing space of music - and which can not be expressed within a framework of pastiche, however well constructed that might be.

Means of access to the personal within the containing space is my discovery in composition teaching, and it seems to me to be similar in some respects to that which is potentially accessible within an analytic frame. So how did I reach this conclusion? Because it is impossible in a school classroom situation to consistently

---

[1] Dunn, R, 'Teaching Music through Individual Composition: A Music Course for Pupils aged Eleven to Eighteen', British Journal of Music Education (1992), **9**, p. 49—60.

teach only one pupil at a time, it is essential to find extra-class time to mentor young composers individually, which I was pleased to do. I was acutely conscious of the extremely delicate nature of these one-to-one working relationships (which often resulted in relatively sophisticated compositions), because I was clearly awakening the students' self-awareness. I was also working without a background of psychoanalytic theory upon which to draw, and any creative successes as a result of my relationships with the students came from intuitive management of their potential .But without exception, though in varying degrees, these young composers responded well at first to the atmosphere of mutual trust, in which my aim of allowing greater freedom for their 'own voice' in composition could be realised. This state of affairs calls to mind the transference situation in analysis, for a 'positive transference' (and counter-transference) is easy to recognise in the co-operative, expectant dialogue between teacher and student during the early one-to-one encounters. However, a mutually painful negativity always seems to arise at some point, for there is no doubt that unconscious conflicts are aroused and acted out in the search for resolution of problems centring on the development of compositional ideas. Two examples illustrate this well.

Jane became interested in composing her own music at about the age of fourteen. An excellent pianist and viola player, but deeply introverted and lacking friends (she was on medication for depression), she was improvising at the piano one day and I suggested that she capture her ideas by notating them. I spent a lot of time with her, talking to her and discussing her work, which was prolific, but she continually drew back from any suggestion that she adopt a more dissonant style to balance what she called her 'beautiful music'. I listened while Jane described her depression (I do not remember verbatim) as: 'staring into a sea of blackness - walking through black mud and struggling to get out'. I intuited that allowing some unresolved dissonance in her music might be expressive of this despair, and might help to alleviate, but I may have been wrong, for she once rounded on me with uncharacteristic anger: '...all you like are bangs and crashes!' Sadly, although Jane went on to study composition at University, her insistence on writing 'beautiful music' was not treated sympathetically; she had a breakdown and ceased to compose altogether. I am now aware not only that for Jane music, as a containing space, was defensive,

A Sound Idea

cloacal, and thus failing as a resource, but also that for composers, performers and listeners, dissonance resonates at a deeply personal level.

My second example, Harriet, began composing at the age of eleven, and at aged fifteen, began to request some of my time for individual help. Her music was then an ebullient pastiche of Rachmaninov - but ideas spilled out onto the page one after the other, far too quickly to be fully absorbed and appreciated by the listener. Yet it was a long time before she acknowledged the desirability of providing her music first with an emotional climax, and then for it to be imbued with her own personality. The turning point for her work came when, after a particularly despairing session, she went home and (according to her sister) pounded the piano in her anger at me! Fortunately, she happened to strike a certain group of notes by accident and, apparently enjoying their dissonance, wrote them down. At her next session, I suggested that this group of notes might be the basis of a composition - she wrote a fifteen-minute, contrapuntal, dissonant, movement for string quartet and it won her a major composition prize. I might now recognise the plenitude of undifferentiated affect contained in Harriet's musical space, which was also failing as a resource. There was a formlessness in her compositions, until in the negative transference she played out (literally!) the oedipally-primed conflicts relating to her own need to differentiate. Thereafter, she adventurously incorporated controlled, dissonant sounds into her music.

I have suggested that music has a role as an unconscious containing space separable from its role in the conscious, measurable order of things. In this role, music attracts emotional affect, then enfolds it and entraps it, from whence it is accessible as musical symbols, vibrant with multi-cultural transcriptional possibilities. Every culture has its music of affect - music to soothe, to entrance, inspire or stimulate. Every music has its mystique - that which cannot be measured. There is a role for music as a collective containing space, thus making sense of the phenomena of non-verbal linguistic utterances of affect being understood by different peoples, through the common symbolism of the rise and fall, strength or volume of vocalised sound, as in murmurs of appreciation or snarls of disapproval. But in any event, the container has to exist prior to the contained, and it must be a suitable container for its contents. Thus, if music is understood simply as elements of sound, it can be appreciated just how early in the life of a human being the process of constructing such a containing space begins. In an embryo, the internal hearing apparatus develops before the apparatus of sight, being almost complete as early as 36 days, and we know that the intrauterine sound-world is of great importance (a congenitally deaf child will continue the embryonic mode of appreciating sound as vibration). However, experiments have shown that the fetus does not regard all sound-impingement with equanimity, for the fetal heart rate increases (it is assumed, as a result of distress) as the affect of certain sound-experiences is discharged by the sympathetic nervous system.[2] Seldom, however, is any consideration given to the possibility of long-term psychic effect of sound-impingement upon the developing sensate being.

From psycho-acoustics, inferences can be drawn about the nature of sound-impingement upon the fetus which assist appraisal of their effect. Certain sounds resonate sympathetically (in mathematical proportion) with the physical body and others do not. Musically speaking, the first are perceived as consonant and the second as dissonant. A different categorisation of sound-impingement separates the soothing, omni-present maternal sounds, from those sounds which cause foetal distress. In the latter category (all of which would cause the fetus some surprise as they occurred) a further distinction can be drawn between those which can be habituated, and those whose qualities of timbre, loudness or randomness preclude habituation. The fetus is thus involved in a process of sound-differentiation based on an absolute lack of cognition. Pre-cognitive experiences are of vital importance in psychoanalysis because, lacking any verbal referents, their mnemic traces lie at the heart of the individual psyche.

It is also possible to suggest a dual psychic effect of those sound-experiences which are responsible for the greatest amount of affect. Not only might they induce a traumatic state (narcissistic wounds) by virtue of the limited capacity of the fetus to tolerate them, but they might also be a primary differentiating medium for the pre-natal Self. However, the pre-nate's qualitative categorisation of sound-impingement is suggestive of a coping mechanism which treats each category as a separate part-object (perhaps as benevolent, tolerable or malevolent/persecutory) with crucial conse-

---

[2] Piontelli, A, From Fetus to Child, Tavistock/Routledge, 1992.

A Sound Idea

quences.[3] It is this primitive human response to sound which possibly awakens sound's immanent potential to receive the unconscious projections of emotional affect (thereby making music appear either benevolent, tolerable or malevolent/persecutory). Therefore a self-perpetuating system is initiated, whereby emotional affects of sound-experiences are projected on to later experiences of music. Music would then be primed to continue to receive projections of emotional affect, including those emotional affects not induced exclusively by sound. This, the process of attraction, enfolding and entrapment, partly constitutes the role of music as a containing space (it remains for the discharge of affects to be addressed). This containing space is constructed over a period of time by the accumulation of its own content of mnemic traces, and is placed within the parameters and dictates of the post-natal unconscious.

That which has arrived in the psyche from a sensuous, pre-natal sound-experience is destined to re-sound emotionally as an individual's 'poetic truth', and collectively re-sound as the mystique of music - unconscious and untranslatable as such. But through the mediating role of symbols, mnemic traces are transcribed into organised musical sound and discharged from music's containing space into consciousness - primal affects fulfilling a potential. Sounds organised as musical configurations are affective by virtue of their symbolism in the individual composer's private discourse of affect; and they are collectively affective as cultural norm-referents, such as pitch-rise and tempo-increase being indicative of an increase in tension. Thus, more can be understood of a young composer's 'need to be heard' by the acceptance of dissonance as an essential musical device, for dissonance is deeply expressive of the differentiating self, and of the composer's identification with pre-natal lived experience which is denied verbal articulation. As Theodor Adorno writes in Aesthetic Theory:

> 'Expression in works of art is the non-subjective in the subject: it is not so much the subject's expression as it is its impression, in the sense of imprint.'[4]

---

[3] It is interesting to note in this context that the composer Richard Rodney Bennett spoke recently of his choice of chords in a composition having the status of 'found objects'.
[4] Adorno, T W, Aesthetic Theory (1970) Trans. C. Lenhardt, Routledge and Kegan Paul 1984, p. 165.

I would be inclined to add: '...the invasion of the non-subjective in the subject...'

To return to the concept of 'trauma', and the possibility of a narcissistic wound to the vulnerable, pre-natal Self. I am reminded of that most remarkable slow movement in the Fourth Piano Concerto of Beethoven, composed in 1806 when his deafness was already well advanced. It is unique in form, being cast in the nature of a dialogue between the assertive strings of the orchestra and the placatory piano solo, during which each interrupts the other several times. As the movement draws to a close, the strings are divested of their aggression and the piano has the last, quiet word. I have long wondered what compensatory mechanism in Beethoven's mind lay behind the conversational structure of this movement, but which in addition lies behind the cadenza-like passages appearing in his piano sonatas from 1802, and the beginning of the final movement of the Ninth Symphony (although the latter is more obviously context-related). Quite clearly, that which is not measurable in the music is that which intrigues, and prompts recourse to psychoanalytic theory. Therefore it can be posited that the onset of Beethoven's deafness necessitated a cathartic abreaction, or 'working out' in successive compositions in order to avoid a pathological melancholia - a process which finds expression in trauma theory. Mnemic traces of the original affective state, later 'bound' to his deafness were symbolised by Beethoven in such a way as to be understood as conversational elements in his music.

A reverse process takes place in music therapy where, through musical symbolism, long-term psychic distress or more recent experiences manifesting behavioural 'affects' is alleviated. Broadly speaking, in a dialogue with the patient, the therapist initiates a series of improvisations which, in the manner of word-association, assists the patient's recall of affective events. Due to the possibility of pre-natal traumatic sound experience being at the heart of psychic pain, music therapy is admirably suited to healing the narcissistic wound. For example, a few years ago I was working once a week with children with special needs, and particularly with Valerie, a frail six-year-old with cri du chat syndrome.[5] Valerie loved the electronic keyboard, and being enabled to reach the keys, after

---

[5] Dunn, R, 'Music: a Shared Experience', British Journal of Special Education (1992), 19:3, p. 109—111.

A Sound Idea

many weeks she discovered that if she held down two adjacent notes at once, a dissonant sound could be made to last for as long as she chose. Holding the dissonance, she would raise and lower her head and wriggle her feet excitedly. One day, with the dissonant sound filling the room, and with unusually focused expression, she looked me straight in the eye, and held my gaze for some time. What was the dissonance 'saying' to her, that she should wish to communicate so directly to me? The mathematically unsynchronised vibrations of dissonance set up a 'beat' in the air, particularly discernible over such a period of time as Valerie preferred; though I have no idea what its 'poetic truth' was for her, I did come to realise that the jumble of classroom noise was distressing for her, and that the even 'beat' of dissonance was not.

Placing psychoanalysis at the service of music or vice versa, highlights an urgent need to make theoretical clarifications out of assumptions, and there is a relatively small, but growing number of writers involved in the discourse, the diverse nature of whose work is roughly represented by the two volumes of Psychoanalytic Explorations in Music.[6] However it is disappointing to find that, though musicology has almost gained its just credence as a science and is applied well in this context, the concept of the unconscious, so crucial to psychoanalysis, only receives one indexed reference in the first volume and four in the second! Without theoretical clarifications it remains all too easy to dismiss musico/psychoanalytic hypotheses as mere projections from the unconscious mind of the writer. Nevertheless, it is difficult to challenge music's primal position in the natural order, making its complex relationship to the psyche a many-faceted scrutiny which will continue to place psycho-biological and psycho-acoustical research at its heart. But to reach an understanding of music's mystique involves the establishment of a fresh hermeneutic - an imperative study for which I have scarcely laid the first foundations here.

---

[6] Feder, M, Karmel, R, and Pollock, G, (Eds), Psychoanalytic Explorations in Music, International Universities Press, volume 1 (1990), volume 2 (1993).

ACKNOWLEDGEMENTS

I acknowledge the ever-present assistance and support of my husband, Clive Dunn; also the helpful criticism of Paul Hardy, musician and linguist, and the encouragement of Dr Martin Stanton, David Reason and Tessa Fineman, music adviser.

Genealogy of the Museum: John Bargrave's Cabinet in context

Stephen Bann

In a moving essay published to commemorate Goethe during the First World War, Freud writes of the custom of 'mourning over the loss of something that we have loved or admired'.[1] In this text which clearly anticipates his later study of mourning, he ponders over the effects of war, which strips us of the objects to which the libido is attached. Yet he also expresses the conviction that these objects can be replaced. 'When it has renounced everything that has been lost, then it has consumed itself, and our libido is once more free ... to replace the lost objects by fresh ones equally or still more precious'. This brief meditation of Freud made me think again about a question which had concerned me intermittently ever since I began to work on the general field of the historical consciousness of the early nineteenth century, and in particular on the collecting habits of Alexandre du Sommerard, founder of that pioneering historical museum, the Musée de Cluny.[2] Having accepted the pertinence of Foucault's claim that such historical mindedness was essentially a reaction to a sense of loss - to the sense of being 'dispossessed of history' - I was obliged to think in particularly concrete terms about the activities of a figure like Du Sommerard. Was it possible, and fruitful to think of Du Sommerard's painstaking assembly of objects hitherto accorded no status, and his creation of a permanent context for their exhibition, as a strategy of historical recovery? Was the resonance which the Musée de Cluny achieved in the 1830's and 40's a measure of the fact that the reinvention of history, so to speak, took place against the general context of a mourning for its loss?

---

[1] Freud, S, Art and Literature (Harmondsworth: Penguin books, 198), p. 288.
[2] Cf. Stephen Bann, The Clothing of Clio (Cambridge: Cambridge University Press, 1984), pp. 77-92; and The Inventions of History (Manchester: Manchester University Press, 1990), pp. 122-47.

Teaching Transference

This question seemed to require comparative examples in order to take its investigation further. In particular, I was wary of looking at 'case histories' from the some period as Du Sommerard since they could all too easily be made to fit the same pattern. I had to keep open my view of what a 'collection', or a 'museum' might amount to, as an expression of individual or collective meaning within a specific historical context. Freud was useful once again in this respect. As the recent touring exhibition of objects drawn from the Freud Museum has made amply clear, he collected voraciously enough to fill any number of museum showcases. But his aim was certainly not to add one more extension to some gallery of Greek and Egyptian antiquities. His cult of objects was determined, in general terms, by the fact that he saw archaeology as a potent metaphor for the activity of bringing to the surface what the conscious mind had decided to repress. His practical use of objects was governed (as the precious testimony of the poet H.D. informs us) by the conjunctural requirements of the individual analysis. That barricade of antique statuettes which stood along the back of his desk could be mobilised to illustrate a cultural reference - to Athena, or Eros - in the dialectical exchange between analyst and analysand.

So it was a question of looking at the historical circumstances of the genesis of a collection, but doing so in such a way that the use of objects - their value and their significance from the collector's point of view - as not predetermined by social conventions. This inevitably implied returning to a stage not only before the museum in its specifically modern sense, but also before the development of the habits of collecting which preceded and to a great extent predetermined it (Du Sommerard's Museum was in this sense a development anticipated in the antiquarian cult of objects which began in the mid-18th century).

It implied returning to a kind of zero degree of collecting - collecting when there was no tradition of collection to follow, and the historical and cultural circumstances could thus be analysed more fruitfully in order to give this bizarre activity its widest possible resonance. Obviously this was an ambition which could not be carried out in conceptually perfect experimental conditions. But it might be possible to find an example so rich in its individuality, and so diverse in its historical connections, that the practical side of collecting would diminish to a great degree, and its symbolic side

Genealogy of the Museum

be revealed. The Museum would be revealed not as an 'invention', ex nihilo, but as a symbolic construction mediating thought and memory, the product of specific historical conditions but itself an irreversible factor in the development of cultural awareness.

In proposing the Cabinet of John Bargrave as this particular example, I am backing my hunch that his activity as a collector was so remarkably individual as to offer a revelation of this kind. What I am offering is a supplement to a completed book project on the life and career of this mid-17th century English churchman; in fact, this enterprise has ramified more and more as I have tried to define its outer limits. Like one of Bargrave's own faceted crystals, it shows any number of different configurations, according to the position from which it is viewed. Bargrave's eventful like, cut in two by the great lacuna of the Civil War, opens up vistas in the history of his native land which take us far beyond the circumstances even of those momentous years. Yet there is always the Cabinet itself - aptly described in the first modern article on the subject as having been 'to oblivion and back' - to recall us to concreteness.[3]

So Bargrave's 'cabinet of medals, antiquities, rareties, and coynes', bequeathed to the Library of Canterbury Cathedral where it has remained ever since, is the main focus of this presentation. But my particular interest in it starts from another, equally perdurable source: the memorial tablet dated 1663 in Patrixbourne Church which announces itself as being written by John Bargrave to commemorate the deaths of his father and brother in the Civil War, and placed by another John Bargrave, whom we can deduce to have been his nephew. Here a brief summary of our John Bargrave's career may be necessary. Born in 1610 or thereabouts, he was well launched on an ecclesiastical career, and a Fellow of Peterhouse, Cambridge, when, in 1643, his compromising connection with his uncle, the stoutly royalist Dean of Canterbury, led to his summary ejection from the university. He left England shortly afterwards, and repeatedly travelled the continent, amassing his collection among other things, till the Restoration of the monarchy in 1660 enabled him to return. The memorial tablet [Fig. 1] which

---

[3] Cf. John Harris, 'To oblivion and back—Dr Bargrave's Museum of Rarities', Country Life, 30 January 1986, pp 278-81. Bargrave's Cabinet is also mentioned, all too briefly, in Oliver Impey and Arthur Macgregor (eds.), The Origins of Museums (Oxford: Oxford University Press, 1985), pp. 152-53.

you see here starkly records what he found: the Bargrave family has 'stood and fallen in the Civil War on the royal side'; the heir (his nephew) can only place this stone 'from ruins to ruins'.

The conjunction of these two aspects of Bargrave's legacy already seems striking. On the one hand, he leaves to the great, and abiding Church of Christ at Canterbury the collection of objects which he has accumulated in his years of exile, having housed them in a set of three 'cabinets'. On the other hand, he signs himself in mourning (lugens scripsit) as the representative of a family which has 'stood and fallen' in the War. His father has built a great house, named Bifrons, in the parish of Patrixbourne near Canterbury, and so established the family (BIFRONTIS and FAMILIA are the two words capitalised in the inscription). But the War has confounded his intentions, so that his grandson and heir is merely an heir to 'ruins'. It should be mentioned at this point the estate of Bifrons, no doubt encumbered by debt as a result of the family's decline during the Commonwealth, had been sold to a gentleman from the North of England in 1662, the year receding the date of the memorial inscription.

It is hard to resist the hypothesis that Bargrave's collection, as a symbolic construction, was related in some significant way to his membership of this particular family, whose demise he records so plangently. In what sense was the Bargrave family, also, a symbolic construction? This is a question which we might answer in general terms, since to recognise paternity is also to enter the symbolic order, and also in specific terms, since the Bifrons family was a remarkable example of that 'self-fashioning' which Stephen Greenblatt has described a special feature of the late Renaissance. John Bargrave Senior signalled his determination to establish a new personal, and familial identity in at least three ways, First of all, he changed the orthography of his surname from the lowly Barger or Bargar (meaning the master or crewman of a barge) to Bargrave (a name with undoubted aristocratic connotations, as in Margrave, the count of a mark or border territory). Secondly, he endowed the Bargrave family with a coat of arms: from prosperous yeoman stock they acquired 'armigerous' status (see again the inscription) when Camden granted John Senior the right to bear arms in 1611. Thirdly, he supplied his newly named and armigerous family with a country seat, the house of Bifrons which was constructed throughout the childhood of the younger John, our collector.

Genealogy of the Museum

It is important to be quite specific about the significance of this paternity for the younger John. And this implies a brief digression on the life and connections of his formidable father. It seems clear that he attended Cambridge University, matriculating as a fellow commoner from Clare College in Easter 1588 (the year of the Spanish Armada) and admitted to Lincoln's Inn on 7 November 1590. It appears from fascinating document in the records of the Virginia Company (of which I shall have more to say later) that he spent the years 1605 to 1615 serving as a mercenary officer in Flanders in the summer, 'and in my study in the wynter'; from 1616 to 1623, however, he ceased campaigning and devoted himself to his involvement with the newly founded Virginia Company, in which he had a considerable investment.[4] At some stage, probably in the early years of the century, he had married the daughter and co-heiress of a London merchant, Giles Crouch. This no doubt was the beginning of his prosperity, which later increased by the fortunate profits of his war service. The coat of arms granted by Camden alludes directly, with its pheon (or arrowhead) crest, its laurel branch, its sword and its golden bezants, to the fortune to be obtained from successful military exploits.

John Senior's grant of arms should not, of course, be seen as the stuff of individual biography alone. To become armigerous in 1611 was to participate in what has been termed an attempt to 'revitalize English knighthood', aptly symbolised by the chivalric ceremony known as 'Prince Henry's Barriers' held on 11 December 1609 when Inigo Jones and others designed a pageant for the young heir to the throne.[5] The Bargrave family, though of yeoman origins, did not lack court connections, since John's younger brother Isaac (the future Dean of Canterbury) was for some time Chaplain to Prince Charles, who became heir to the throne on Henry's death in 1612. But if the ascent of the Bargraves therefore reflected a particular court ideology during the early Stuart monarchy, it is at the same time legitimate to draw attention to some special features in John Senior's 'self-fashioning'. Other families acquired arms during these years, fulfilling the usual pattern

---

[4] Cf. Susan Kingbury, The Records of the Virginia Company of London (Washington, 1935), Vol. IV, p. 435.

[5] Cf. Stephen Orgel, The Illusion of Power (Berkeley: University of California Press, 1975), pp. 66-70.

whereby the wealth of the City of London was transferred, by means of marriage alliances, into the more prestigious coin of landed property. Other families built great country houses in the vicinity of the Bargrave estate.

The house known as Dene, at Wingham, was built by the ancient family of Oxenden in 1584. Half a century later, in 1635, Sir Basil Dixwell, who had inherited land in Kent from a maternal uncle, built Broome Park, which has been described as 'clearly designed by an architect with knowledge of Inigo Jones's classical style'.[6] The house of Bifrons belongs between these two other examples, both temporally and geographically. But it exemplifies a personal symbolism which is arguably all its own. In the first place, as Hasted noted in his eighteenth-century History of Kent, it bore 'this motto on the fore front: Diruta aedificat uxor bona, aedificata diruit mala'.[7] 'A good wife builds up what has been demolished, a bad wife demolishes what has been built'. Hasted is undoubtedly enunciating a truism when he writes that the builder of Bifrons placed this motto 'in commendation of his wife', and yet the meaning of the phrase is hardly crystal clear. In what sense was Jane Bargrave, nee Crouch, however much her wealth may have contributed to the ascension of her husband's family, 'building up what [had] been demolished'? It is at least possible to see in this motto evidence for a myth which is otherwise without foundation: that John Bargrave Senior believed his family to have had a former standing which it had subsequently lost (though Camden's genealogy does not allow for any such remote and flattering ancestry).

The second sense in which the house may have exemplified a personal symbolism lies in its very name, Bifrons. Again Hasted supplies an interpretation which hold only on the superficial level: it was 'so called from its double front'. I am reluctant to believe that this 'double front' - by which I understand the facade flanked by two projecting bays which is visible in the very fine anonymous early eighteenth-century painting of Bifrons, in the collection of the British Art Centre at Yale - is all that lies behind the house name. John Senior was a learned man, as those winters spent in his

---

[6] Cf. Charles Latham, In English Homes (London, 1909), Vol. III, p. 101.
[7] Edward Hasted, History of the County of Kent (Canterbury, 1800: 1972 reprint), Vol. IX, p. 281.

Genealogy of the Museum

study away from the wars attest; his letters on the affairs of the Virginia Company show a wide familiarity with Greek and Roman history. He would surely have been aware that 'Bifrons' was a epithet conventionally applied to Janus, whose temple at Rome had its doors closed only in time of peace throughout the Roman world. In a poem dated 1 January 1630, the poet Thomas Carew celebrated Charles I's peace with Spain in the previous year with the verses:

> But, Byfront, open thou no more
> In his blest raigne, the temple dore.[8]

It is reasonable to suggest the building of Bifrons around 1615, after he has retired from 'service in the warres', implied for John Bargrave Senior the construction of his own Temple of Janus. If so, there is a particularly cruel irony in the fact that civil war was to wreak havoc on himself and his family only a quarter of a century later, and bring about the downfall of his house.

I have been concentrating on the career of the father of the collector in order to emphasise how overdetermined the paternal order must have been for the young John Bargrave. In my rough and ready definition of 'personal symbolism', I have been differentiating between the visible markers of social prestige which are handed down across the generations and those which are assumed as an integral aspect of the process of 'self-fashioning'. The coat of arms generally belongs to the first category, while the impresa or personal device - so popular among the upper classes in the seventeenth century - belongs to the second. Yet a grant of arms which is given for the first time, and one which clearly records the subject's own prowess, obviously has more the character of a device than of an inherited blason. John Senior marked in the most decisive way, through his change of name, his grant of arms and his building of Bifrons, his own status as a founding father (conditor). John the collector, not the heir but the second son, must have experienced the family as a mythic formation which her inhabited, and yet did not inhabit at the same time. Not the heir, and yet the son who bore his father's name, he must have been aware that he inherited a status which his father's labours had made possible: the

---

[8] Cf. Rhodes Dunlop, Poems of Thomas Carew (Oxford: Oxford University Press, 1949), pp. 89-90.

Teaching Transference

coat of arms which he takes care to feature in his portraits (completed during his exile and later included in the cabinet) is his own by right, and at the same time a legacy granted specifically by his father, The great house, whose building must have been the most momentous event of his childhood, not only concretises his family status, but bears the testimony of his mother's virtues writ across its facade (it is not clear when she died, but her absence from the commemorative text of 1662, and the fact that she had at least four children after John, suggests that she may have died in the decade 1620-30). All these aspects of his family background, in other words, appear to him in his youth as being foregrounded in the symbolic order. And then, with the outbreak of the Civil War, the symbolic order is overturned. His uncle the Dean is the victim of outrage, and the very office of Dean suppressed; after a few years, the King to whom Isaac Bargrave was once chaplain is himself decapitated. John Bargrave starts his travels throughout Europe in the aftermath of this first symbolic loss. Even the Restoration on 1660 does not in any sense restore to him what has been already lost by this stage. The King's son returns, and the Dean and Chapter of Canterbury being reinstituted, he himself is provided with a Canonry in 1662. But the glory of the elder branch of the Bargraves is gone for ever. Uncle to the luckless heir, he decides to create a legacy which will outlast the loss of Bifrons and circumvent his own lack of progeny. He decides to form the objects collected in his long years of exile into a permanent Cabinet, a Museum.

I can envisage all kinds of ways in which this reading of the symbolic antecedents of Bargrave's collection could be criticised and made the subject of debate. The point of the present paper is simply to set up a number of propositions for discussion. I think it very likely for example, that Bargrave Senior's unfortunate investment in the Virginia Company, which leads him to petition constantly for 'losse of my Estate' as early as 1623, had already sensibly diminished the prosperity of Bifrons within a decade of its foundation. Thus the young John would have observed first of all, around five years old, the building of the great house, and then become aware as he proceeded towards adolescence of the precarious state of the family fortune. The experience of the Civil War perhaps only hastened and made definitive the family's downfall from one generation of prominence. I also think that the

Genealogy of the Museum

young John's position as a second son, and his inclination to holy orders, must from an early stage have prepared him to expect no more than a symbolic share of the family wealth: the bezants on the coat of arms, perhaps, but no share in the Patrixbourne estate. And the same time, I find it irresistible to conclude that his experience as a member of the Bargrave family, coupled with his experience as a victim of the Civil War, prepared him to undertake a form of compensation for his loss which was destined to remain securely within the order of the symbolic. Flaubert, in Sartre's biographical account, reacts to the impossible pressures placed upon him by successful professional role models within his family by becoming a neurasthenic and a writer; in contradistinction to his father and brother, he would be not a real dissector, but the anatomist of Madame Bovary. Bargrave, who ended his life married to a wealthy widow, spent so much on the creation of a sumptuous monument to his uncle the Dean in Canterbury Cathedral, that his relict bridled at honouring the debt. But him more enduring legacy was his trio of cabinets - double-fronted, like the house of his father.

By introducing this deliberate anachronism, I want however to draw attention to yet another specific feature of the constraints of paternity which Bargrave must have experienced. He was not, like Flaubert, the child of a bourgeois family, in which the successful professional man imposed, as father, an intolerable burden (if we agree with Sartre's reading). Patriarchalism was more widely diffused in the seventeenth century, and the extended family or household rather than the nuclear family of post-industrial society was the norm. Nonetheless, I want to argue that John Bargrave was exposed, if not to the Oedipal pressure of a modern father, then to the effects of a developing ideology of paternalism in which his own family, and their network of alliances, played a significant part. Peter Laslett has claimed in a pioneering article that the gentry of Kent were indeed of capital importance in propagating an ideology of conservatism and paternalism which was to outlive the circumstances of the Commonwealth period. He notes that on two occasions, when they proceeded en masse to Westminster in March 1642 to present their county petition of grievances (a move which helped to precipitate the taking up of arms) and when they rose against the Parliament in May 1648 to try and rescue the King (a move which resulted in the savage Battle of Maidstone, the last armed confrontation of the war), they were intervening decisively, if unsuccessfully on the royal side. For Laslett, however, this intervention which fails in practice becomes overwhelmingly influential in theory, and not only in Kent itself, but 'in Virginia in the area of the James river' where the Kentish gentry had transplanted their network of alliances. So he is ready to state that the gentry of Kent produced, as a result of their disastrous experience of the Civil War, not only 'the political thinking of Sir Robert Filmer [leading theorist of patriarchal government in late seventeenth-century England]' but also 'the society of the Old South in the United State'.⁹

Laslett's view of Filmer as the ideologist of the Kentish gentry in general has been challenged in recent studies. But this does not really affect my argument. For there is no doubt that the Bargrave family was a new recruit, in the 1620's, to that close-knit group of families who maintained their power through periodic alliance with the great merchant families of London and through the prestige of the Church: Isaac Bargrave was, like most Deans of Canterbury, a scion of a Kentish family and, moreover, he enhanced his position in the structure of power by marrying into the ancient knightly family of Dering. Nor is there any doubt that John Senior, the father of the collector, was a powerful (and original) spokesman for a form of government in Virginia which would have strengthened its links with the English crown, to the extent of annihilating any mediation or colonial status for the newly settled territory. His long statement of 1623 is entitled: 'A Forme of Polisie to Plante and Governe many Families in Virginea, soe as it shall naturally depend one the Soveraignetye of England'.¹⁰ As I understand it, Bargrave's scheme has been given scant attention by American historians, and virtually no attention by British political scientists. But it is not fanciful to imagine that he was speaking for a nascent ideology which was only temporarily obscured by the Civil War. Suffice it to say that, in this policy for Virginia which was produced in concert with members of the Rich family, who were his allies in the Virginia Company, Bargrave Senior is already using the term

---

⁹ Peter Laslett, 'The gentry of Kent in 1640' Cambridge Historical Journal 9 (1948), 148-64. Cf. also Alan Everitt, Kent and the Great Rebellion (Leicester: Leicester University Press, 1966) for a more restricted view of Filmer's importance.

¹⁰ Kinsbury, Records of the Virginia Company, Vol. IV, p.408.

Genealogy of the Museum

of 'Patriote' and 'Lord Patriote' for the paternal authorities of the government of Virginia; the foremost ideologist of paternalism and conservatism in eighteenth-century England was to be Henry St John, Viscount Bolingbroke, grandson of Robert Rich, Earl of Warwick and proponent of the ideal of the 'Patriot King'.

I am not trying to argue that John Bargrave the collector necessarily shared his father's views. What seems undeniable is that he was aware of the close texture of power relations formed by the Kentish gentry, and of the way in which his father was concerned to project those relations, in a Utopian form, into the government of Virginia, where indeed more than one member of the Bargrave family was settled. And this seems to me the clue to the compilation to his other major work, apart from the catalogue of his collection, which was published in the nineteenth century under the title College of Cardinals. As can be seen, Bargrave announces on the fly-leaf that he has assembled these prints of the Roman princes of the Church on his 'fourth and laste time of Rome' in 1660 [fig. 2]. He has, however, embellished the visual record with a remarkably full series of notes on the various figures represented in the prints, which demonstrate a consuming interest in the power relations obtaining within the Eternal City. As Louis Marin has stressed in a recent edition of a political text published in Rome in 1639, the Roman Church was at this time harbouring a particularly sophisticated political culture.[11] Bargrave is no expert in this field, but he does note with special attention the features or the Papal court, writing of Pope Urban VIII: 'Never prince was more absolute in a conquest than the Barbarinos were in their administration of the Church and City of Rome'. Of his two nephews, Bargrave goes on to write: 'Their uncle being Pope xxiii years, in the whole consistory of Cardinals there were but five who were not their creatures; so they, having all the rest at their command, lorded it over the Church and State, and over all Christendom ... as monarchs of the world'.[12] It is as if the nephew of the Dean - the dean who himself represented the centre of a web of power and patronage up to the eve of the Civil War - were dispassionately pondering the spectacle of a power nexus which showed his own

---

[11] Gabriel Naudet, Considerations politiques sur les Coups d'Etat, with an introductory essay by Louis Marin (Paris: Editions de Paris 1988).

[12] John Bargrave, Pope Alexander the Seventh (London: Camden Society, 1867), p. 29.

position displaced and magnified to an extraordinary degree, yet divorced from any practical engagement of himself as spectator.

Of course it is Bargrave's collection and the catalogue accompanying it that form the main focus of my interest in him. These are explored more extensively in my recent book, illustrated with images which display the scope and character of Bargrave's collecting zeal.[13] What I have tried to do in this introductory paper is to fill in the circumstances of John Bargrave's life and, more than that, to indicate how we might begin to think about the position which his collection was designed to fill, in a symbolic order constituted by his social and familial relationships. Bargrave as subject was held within this order, and indeed it is hard to tell his story at all without acknowledging the impressive stature of his father and his uncle, and particularly that precursory John Bargrave who built Bifrons and created a scheme of government of Virginia. I do not want to imply that the collector John Bargrave's life took place, so to speak, in the shadow of these dominant and patriarchal figures. Quite the opposite, I would argue that the necessities of exile during the Civil War impelled him to make his own treaty with the symbolic order, Rome could be studied as the macrocosmic reflection of a remembered (but no longer existent) Canterbury. The Cabinet could be set up and displayed to visitors as a spectacle corresponding to the building and adornment of Bifrons, with its component items having little value in themselves but forming nonetheless a coherent and diversified world: a world of specimens, both animal and mineral - a world of antiquities, both false and authentic - a world of optical transformations and reversals which perhaps provide the best clue to the particular kind of agility (of eye and mind) with which Bargrave transformed the disparate records of his journeying into that simulacrum of permanence which we call a museum.

---

[13] See Under the Sign: John Bargrave as Collector, Traveller, and Witness (Ann Arbor: University of Michigan Press, 1994).

(Fig 1) Bargrave Family Memorial Tablet

(Fig 2) Flyleaf from 'College of Cardinals'

Racism, Incest and Modernity: Everyone is now a stranger among strangers

Christopher Hauke

> 'The price of hating other human beings is loving oneself less.'
>
> Cleaver, E (1968), Soul On Ice,

Introduction: The Social and the Psychological

In the fragmented world of academic discourse a psychological explanation of human phenomena tends to be opposed to a sociological explanation and each view will lay claim to its superior, more powerful 'truth'. Depth psychological views may assume greater validity, for example, by pointing out the absence of the concept of the unconscious in other views. Sociological views may point out the inadequacies in their 'other' by referring to the poor samples and lack of statistical analysis in psychoanalytic explanations. These oppositions of 'self' and 'other' are crudely drawn here, but the elements that constitute such a conceptualising of 'self' and 'other' are regularly present and regularly go unremarked. As a global approach to phenomena, such oppositional thinking is not an optional tool for examining the world, but unconsciously informs, structures and maintains a split perspective. Moreover, this mode of apprehending phenomena is not confined to, or simply a product of, scientific academic thinking; indeed, my point is these discourses have themselves become subject to such a paradigm as modernity has taken its course. The oppositional paradigm expressed as 'self' and 'other' reveals a deep split in the modern psyche, the results of which can be seen enacted daily in modern life through a wide range of psychological and sociological phenomena. One such case is racism.

I have hesitated before mentioning the apparent subject of this paper because there is also another subject here. It is no use analysing the psychic or social/economic schisms that produce racism if the analysing consciousness is making no attempt to address this split in itself. As Paul Gordon puts it in a recent paper:

> 'Psychoanalysis cannot provide a theory of racism, although it can - and should - be part of one. Racism is in the material world as well as the psyche and our attempt to understand it ... must be in two places at once.'[1]

Racism is always an individual, affect laden experience no doubt contributed to by an individual's varying personal capacity to deal with hostility, aggression and difference. But it is also a social phenomenon that has powerful political, economic and cultural effects. It has a history in European nations and various forms of racism have contributed and continue to contribute materially to the type of civilisation we enjoy now and the political and economic shape of the world as we know it. Racism is an individual experience contextualised by the collective social-political experience. More than this, like gender, it is informed by the collective and structured by the collective at an unconscious level. As Franz Fanon bluntly put it in 1967, 'The myth of the bad nigger is part of the collective unconscious'.[2]

A way of imagining these 'two places' might be to see each, the social and the psychological, as filters for each other. Social racism is filtered through specific psychological phenomena to produce individual behavioural phenomena in the form of an Enoch Powell, a violent BNP activist, or a paternalistic slave-owner in the 1830s. Equally, changing social structures, economic needs and political values are filtered through individual psychology to produce the present fragmented and tense situation where anti-racist legislation exists side-by-side with persistent racial discrimination. This can be explained by viewing the apparent consensus of the democratic state as always being filtered by differentiated individual responses to the non-white minority.

In this paper I wish to follow Gordon's recomendation of analysing racism from the 'two places', the individual and the collec-

---

[1] Gordon, P (1993) 'Souls in Armour; Thoughts on Psychoanalysis and Racism', British Journal of Psychotherapy, **10**, 1, p. 73.
[2] Fanon, F (1967), Black Skin, White Masks, Granada, London in Brown, P (1973) Radical Psychology, Tavistock, London, pp. 267-8.

tive, the psychological and the social. But in addition, I aim to stay conscious of the unconscious splitting that imposes a 'self' and 'other' onto our experience and forces us into oppositional modes of thinking. In this case I will be using what Jung has to say about the function of the opposites in the human psyche and the meaning of the incest symbol.

I am influenced by Jung's views, and especially their relevance when linked to the analysis of modernity, but I also follow Andrew Samuels in seeking 'to insert depth psychology sensitively into a discourse where it has not been present....(because)...to be indirect is a particular contribution of depth psychology - a grasp on reflection and an ability to deepen any issue that it touches'.[3] My second aim is to develop Samuel's position where he is citing the need for a psychology of difference that can explain the power of the opposites - not simply accept or reject them but to discover their political force.[4] My third aim concerns the subversive potential of depth psychology within the thrust towards a resacralisation of culture, and the function of the margin.[5]

Racism, some definitions.

Before I continue I need to clarify various points about my use of the word 'racism'. Firstly, I hold that 'race' itself is an empty category that cannot refer to any biological or genetic difference between peoples that is anything more than trivial. It is an often repeated point that there is far more individual difference within any delineated racial group than there are average differences between such groups.[6] Despite the superficiality of the visible differences between races in terms of skin-colour and facial features, these take on huge importance as markers, as the identifying characteristics

---

[3] Homans, P (1979), Jung in Context; Modernity and the Making of a Psychology, University of Chicago Press, Chicago; Samuels, A(1993), The Political Psyche, Routledge: London, p. 76.
[4] Samuels, A, The Political Psyche, pp. 328-329.
[5] Samuels, A, The Political Psyche, p. 76.
[6] For example Plomin, P (1994), 'Gene rebels with a cause', The Independent, 20/10/1994

(along with diet etc.) that select a group out for discrimination and oppression. I agree with Rustin when he writes of 'The arbitrariness and baselessness of racial categories,' which makes possible their embodiment as 'pure spirit of otherness'.[7] It is the selection of a group for discrimination that constitutes racism, not any inferiority constituted through difference the group may carry for the racist.

Secondly, this paper is only concerned with the European people's (including those who now form the USA) political, economic and psychological development that has involved a particular racism in this epoch. I am sure that other racisms always persist elsewhere and in other times, and these may be sensitive to other forms of analysis such as in *Purity and Danger*, for example, where Mary Douglas discusses group identity via dietary prohibitions.[8] But racism persisting in other parts of the world, apparently unconnected to the European experience, can often be found to have direct links back to colonial times in addition to the contemporary influence exerted through the World Bank and aid agencies. It was a well known strategy of European colonisation to use existing divisions, discriminations, and enmities, in the indigenous populations to foster greater overall control despite a relatively minimal white presence. Franz Fanon analyses this as the 'racial distribution of guilt' which stems from the whites and moves between ethnic groups such as Jew-Arab, Asian-Negro, African-Caribbean and so on.[9] In this view Fanon emphasises the hegemony of a world system dominated by white Europeans, even when the Europeans are no longer present in person. The distinction between a universalistic and a non-universalistic epoch is commented on by Joel Kovel who notes that only in the former does the cruelty and domination between peoples penetrate into the 'essence of personhood' that we see in slavery and the Holocaust.[10]

Lastly, I believe racism in European culture is more than its gross expression in overtly racist views and actions. It is a manifestation of the sustained splitting of the psyche that constitutes modernity and everyday life. By participating in the culture we participate in

---

[7] Rustin, M (1991), The Good Society and the Inner World, Routledge, London, p. 62.
[8] Douglas, M (1966), Purity and Danger, Penguin, Harmondsworth.
[9] Fanon, F (1967), Black Skin, White Masks, p. 280.
[10] Kovel, J (1988), The Radical Spirit, Free Associations, London.

racism despite our individual position. Evidence for this can be found in facts such as the continuing under-representation of non-white people in professional positions and as university students relative to the population; the over-representation of non-whites in lower paid and service jobs; and the over-representation of non-white males, as unemployed, in prison, excluded from school or diagnosed with serious mental illness. This distortion could not occur except through ideologies, resting on unconscious processes and conscious ideation, that marks non-whites as inferior and circumscribes their freedom to enter the dominant culture without its permission.

Psychoanalysis and Racism

Earlier psychoanalytic attempts at an analysis of racism were characterised by a reductive approach that took little account of the social context or historical aspects of racism, as though it could be understood in intrapsychic or developmental terms alone.[11] In such studies, racism tended to be reduced to the projection and displacement of infantile hatred, hostility or disgust, with the focus restricted to the dynamics of the instincts and the dynamics within the family.

Subsequent analyses have developed from the impetus of the Frankfurt School, especially Adorno, where modernity was examined using Freudian concepts within a Marxist critique of capitalism. The particular form of racism examined is often anti-Semitism, and the key theme in major texts is that modernity provides the individual with an experience that feels insecure, fragmented and alienating. The psychoanalytical point in this analysis

---

[11] For example Sterba, R (1947), 'Some psychological factors in Negro race-hatred and in anti-Negro riots', in G Roheim (ed.), Psychoanalysis and the Social Sciences; Dollard, J (1937), Caste and Class in a Southern Town, Yale University Press, and (1938), 'Hostility and Fear in Social Life', Social Forces, Vol. 17; Orr, D W (1946), 'Anti-semitism and the psychopathology of everyday life', in E. Simnel (Ed.), Anti-Semitism: A Social Disease, International Universities Press, New York; Hamilton, J (1966), 'Some dynamics of anti-Negro prejudice', Psychoanalytic Review, 53; all described fully in Gordon, P (1993) 'Souls in Armour'.

is that racism is seen as a defence against an unbearable sense of alienation. What is key about this phase of psychoanalytical accounts of racism is that the analysis has moved on from the personal experience (i.e. in terms of family dynamics) towards attempting to take fuller account of the modern social context. As Stephen Frosh puts it, these views carry the notion that 'racism is a manifestation of flight from the experience of modernity'.[12]

A further example of this view is demonstrated by Joel Kovel. Sticking closely to the Marxist analysis of capitalism he describes modern psychological and social processes as the result of, and through the metaphor of, the capitalist system of production and exchange. Thus:

> 'Capital is inherently penetrative; its power necessarily extends to the destruction of autonomous cultural bases and, with these, coherent identities. Under the role of capital the self becomes problematised for the first time in world history: people begin not to know who they are. Contemporary racism must be understood as a reflection of this process - and critically, as a defence against it.'[13]

Franz Fanon, writing in the late 1960s, holds views that develop the psychoanalytic perspective more in the direction of my present paper. He provides a critique of *Prospero and Caliban; Psychology of Colonisation*, a book by Mannoni which argues for the psychological idea of a dependency complex in colonised peoples. Fanon encounters in Mannoni the mistaken view that the responsibility for racism lies with 'racists'. Mannoni expresses it as:

> 'European civilisation and its best representatives are not, for instance, responsible for colonial racism; that is the work of petty officials, small traders, and colonials who have toiled much without great success.'[14]

By reducing the problem to one of individuals his view fails to grasp the bigger psychological and historical point of the linkage between racism and the psyche of modernity. In criticising this

---

[12] Frosh, S (1989), 'Psychoanalysis and Racism', in B. Richards (ed.) *Crises of the Self; Further Essays on Psychoanalysis and Politics*, Free Associations, London, p. 235.

[13] Kovel, J (1988), The Radical Spirit, p. 238.

[14] Mannoni, O (1964), Prospero and Caliban: the Psychology of Colonisation, Praeger, New York, p. 8.

more-or-less reductive psychoanalytic position, Fanon also refers to the collective unconscious as the location of contemporary, as well as ancient, collective contents such as 'the myth of the bad nigger' previously mentioned, while also emphasising that 'there are inner relationships between consciousness and the social context'.[15]

Much of what I contribute in my present paper will be seen to broadly agree with Fanon's views; but in writing from a Jungian perspective and outside the Freud-Marx sphere of analysis there will be seen to be important differences. Analytical psychology, I believe, provides a critical edge to discussions that seek to involve the psychological and the social simultaneously. This is because the Jungian conception of the psyche contains the idea of a collective unconscious, as well as the personal unconscious. This provides a way of thinking about the dynamics between the individual and the collective, the psychological and the social, that are already located in a dynamic interplay within each individual. In addition, the concept of the collective unconscious directly addresses the reality of a political and cultural dynamic as a force in itself. In psychoanalytic theorising, the dynamics of social collective behaviour tend to be explained in terms of the dynamics of the ego and id, on the one hand, and the dynamics within the nuclear family, on the other. Psychoanalytic accounts of racism seem dominated by the presence of individual dynamics which are then generalised to form the 'social' effect - or, in other words, collective dynamics are being treated as if they are reducible to the dynamics of individuals.

I find this psychoanalytic approach demonstrated in the constant reference to 'racists', the actors in society who apparently carry the racism and cause it to be a troubling factor.[16] What this perspective misses is the degree to which racism is not the 'passion' (to use Sartre's word coined by Rustin) of certain individuals or groups, but it is part of the ground of modernity. Racism, I will argue, persists ubiquitously and invisibly as one manifestation, among many, of the split psyche of modernity. On the other hand, 'racists' constitute an extreme expression of racism acted-out by individuals,

---

[15] Fanon, F (1967), Black Skin, White Masks, in ; Brown, Radical Psychology, pp. 267-8; Brown, Radical Psychology, p. 273.

[16] Frosh, S, 'Psychoanalysis and Racism' and Rustin, M, The Good Society and the Inner World.

and in individualised behaviour. 'Racists' are more about the violence, aggression and hatred that is being expressed; they are using racism as a vehicle and as a provider of a circumscribed target, a clearly defined 'other', for their animosity. My point is that a Freudian approach will always tend to refer to individuals in explaining the social because its tools of analysis involve individual dynamics in an encounter with the collective. This is in contrast to a Jungian approach which starts with the conceptual advantage of the collective unconscious within the individual psyche, which is produced by and also produces and reproduces collective social forms.

Self and Otherness

It has struck me how young children up to about six practically never remark on the racial difference of other children, but at nine years can be as racist and biased as an adult. This suggests to me two things: firstly, that the developing infant only takes on as much 'otherness' as it can manage at a time. Indeed, research on neurological capacities early in life suggests that the brain paces its capacities for knowing the other - newborn babies are 'actively and effectively avoidant of experiences, and this is particularly noticeable in unfamiliar circumstances'.[17] But secondly, that once a cognitive and emotional capacity for otherness has been established - object constancy with its own individual hierarchy of significant others - social and cultural forces impose a further hierarchy of otherness via ideology and learning.

Attention has also been drawn to certain concepts in contemporary depth psychology that seem to reinforce assumptions of individuals' essential separation from one another that the paradigm of self and other implies. Andrew Samuels points out the weakness inherent in Object Relations theory and especially the concept of projective identification. He points out that the bias in this view suggests that

---

[17] Richard L Gregory, with O.L. Zangwill (1987), Oxford Companion to the Mind, Oxford University Press, Oxford, p. 364.

> 'People are not fundamentally connected in this vision of things; ... this ignoring of communality and communion in the name of communication is not politically neutral ... the concept of projective identification just does not get hold of the collectivity of persons, of where they are already joined together on a psychosocial level, of where things are shared.'[18]

Samuels uses this to argue that projective identification is therefore a relatively weak tool of political analysis, which helps us to understand more accurately the inadequacies of previous psychoanalytical approaches to racism. But it also directs us towards the psychic split sustained by the paradigm of self and other, upon which concepts such as projective identification are based.

I would like to surmise this: it seems that when we make distinctions of otherness, the distance of other from self and the *distance between the others* will be conditioned by certain parameters. Firstly, the cognitive and emotional capacity to register the distinction. Secondly, the range of others available, and thirdly, their valuing or ordering in importance. This is where we have to shift into social theorising - the culture will set the priorities and range of its 'other'. Within this, different contexts, or questions asked will determine where is self or where is other. Lastly, the need of the individual or the culture becomes a factor. This is a central and complex factor which this paper as a whole is trying to address - but for the time being I would put it crudely that the creation of and dealing with the 'other', the Not-self, leads to discomfort and restlessness, to an energy that is always seeking resolution in action and rationality. It is the motor of our present consciousness and a limiter on alternative developments.

The Roots of the Racially Other

The paradigm of self and other which persists in modern thinking is useful in considering how racism grew and now persists in modern times. My main point, which I pick up later when I turn to Jung's theorising on the opposites, is that the paradigm of self and

---

[18] Samuels, A (1993), The Political Psyche, Routledge, London, pp. 276-7.

other replaces and attempts to compensate for a more fundamental dualism or split: that between the unconscious and the conscious mind.

Considered historically, the last five hundred years of European civilisation have seen a consolidation in the breakdown in dialogue between the conscious and the unconscious - frequently depicted as the gulf between 'man' and 'nature'. Early on, this psychological condition was enacted in the political world by elite classes wrenching instrumental power from the Church, and hence from God, and thereby legitimising their new rationalism. Instead of man being the object of God, the material world could be created as the object of man - to achieve, in Schiller's phrase, the 'de-godding of nature'. Through this, Nature could 'be capable of human use and control according to human whim and desire, and Europeans, uniquely as far as we know, among all cultures could assume, in Descartes' words, that humans were "the masters and possessors of nature".[19]

This objectifying in the service of instrumental-rationality, this creation of the exploitable Other, provided the psychological basis for the expansion of Europeans and what we now experience as modernity. It is easy to see how the state of mind that viewed new lands purely in terms of what wealth could be appropriated for use back in Europe, could extend this attitude to the native populations encountered. In this way the European invader was able to view fellow human beings through the binoculars of a secular pragmatism - free of any moral constraint that might have interrupted their ruthless exploitation.

The same rationality that was to be the ground of the Enlightenment meant the shift from God's will to the will of the nation-state and its newly capitalised adventurers - resulting in the establishment of an Other in the exploited populations and resources of far-away lands. The chronicles of perhaps the most famous adventurer, Christopher Columbus, can supply us with expressive detail revealing an individual psychological attitude which confirms this collective historical perspective.

Admiral Colon, Christopher Columbus, in his own and in his contemporaries writings from the period of his voyages between 1492 and 1502, reveals the ramshackle beginnings of such suc-

---

[19] Sale, K (1992), The Conquest of Paradise, Macmillan, London, p. 40.

Racism, Incest and Modernity

cessful exploitation but also typifies the rapidly established racist attitudes that made it possible. When encountering the Taino people on his first landing in 1492, Columbus remarked on their simplicity and friendliness in terms that would later produce ideas of the 'Noble Savage' of the later European imagination; but he immediately presumed their inferiority 'not merely because (a sure enough sign) they were naked, but because (his society could have no surer measure) they seemed so technologically backward. '....very poor in everything,' he wrote, 'they have no iron'.[20] Their pleasant, welcoming nature was also treated cynically with 'they ought to be good servants.....I will carry six off at my departure' and: 'They are fit to be ordered about and made to work.....no Christian need do a hand's turn of work in the Indies'.[21] In this way slavery was born, not intentionally though any rational plan, but as the result of a tribute system so cruelly and hamfistedly enforced that it rapidly disintegrated into full enslavement as the Spanish continued to pursue further gains.

Such ruthlessness led to the fleeing of natives as the colonies began to establish themselves under the Spanish. Natives only fled to live in the hills once the colonists had destroyed their villages and social cohesion, but a retreat to the 'wilds' from long established social organisations enabled the sanctioning of an alternative European image - that of the 'Savage Beast'. The Noble Savage, on the other hand, was characterised as the individual free of the need of interfering government because he was himself free of crime and greed and living in harmony. It is ironic that he should have 'provided the underlying characteristics of the free commonwealth', a Utopian future for a degenerated Europe in the New (Other) World when the image was always entwined with that of the Savage Beast.[22] As Sale says, the latter view of the native took over, 'as soon as anything of real value was seen in the new lands that were inconveniently in the hands of the natives', and especially after Cortes discovered gold in 1519.[23]

---

[20] Sale, K, The Conquest of Paradise, p. 96.
[21] Sale, K, The Conquest of Paradise, p. 97; quoted in Sale, K, The Conquest of Paradise, p. 112.
[22] Sale, K, The Conquest of Paradise, p. 200.
[23] Sale, K, The Conquest of Paradise, p. 201.

Machiavelli in 1513, through to Galileo in 1632, and Descartes in 1637 and 1641, produced, despite the tenuous grip of Rome, the intellectual and philosophical texts that fore-shadowed modernity and began to formalise the necessary split between psyche and the material world of 'nature'. Intellectual expansion followed on from political expansion and economic success and eventually the 18th century saw a 'period of great and exaggerated admiration for the observation of matter and nature'.[24] Nature objectified as Other was established in the Encyclopaedia (written between 1751 and 1764) which was designed to replace Thomas Aquinas' Summa Theologica, and extended European man's mapping of the world previously contoured by God and the Catholic Church.

In America, the Declaration of Independence on the 4th of July 1776 was based on John Locke's 'social contract'. The thinking behind this, ironically inspired by the Utopian image of the Noble Savage, was designed purely for the bourgeoisie to refute the sovereign being able to put himself above the law. Despite its 'all men are created equal and are endowed by their Creator with certain inalienable rights....life, liberty and the pursuit of happiness' the Declaration was far from a liberal distribution of power to the masses. The emphasis on bringing the sovereign within the fully secular realm of government is a continuation of the epoch's earlier steps in splitting from the church and its power. And the blatant hypocrisy of its wording in the context of colonial slavery and the genocide of Native Americans only underlines how simultaneous, and integral to this development, racism has been.

This is the historical and cultural trajectory of modernity, but what of its psychology? I approach this via a consideration of Jung's theories of the Shadow and the Opposites.

The Shadow

I began by describing the general concept of self and other and went on to emphasise the development of a hierarchy of others. My last pages have underlined the construction of self and other where the Other is made inferior with a consequent superiority

---

[24] Sale, K, The Conquest of Paradise, p. 50.

Racism, Incest and Modernity

accruing to self. So much is evident in the case of racism. As Paul Gordon quotes,

> 'By attributing a population with certain characteristics in order to categorise and differentiate it as Other, those who do so establish criteria by which they themselves are represented......by using the discourse of race to exclude and inferiorise, that same discourse.....serves to include and superiorise'.[25]

At the level of individual psychology, Jung defined the shadow as 'the thing a person has no wish to be', and 'the less it is embodied in the individual's conscious life, the blacker and denser it is.'[26] As an archetype, the shadow's contents contain powerful affects which can be projected, and within his theory,

> 'Jung found a convincing explanation not only of personal antipathies but also the cruel prejudices and persecutions of our time.'[27]

Therefore, it has been all too easy to view racism as a mass projection by the dominant white culture onto the black population, the whites having identified a group to carry their shadow. This level of explanation can be useful, especially in certain areas. I am thinking of the themes of materiality and sexuality where it can be viewed that the shadow of capitalist acquisitiveness and greed gets projected as black criminality, and the shadow of instinctive sexuality gets projected on to the black male as rapist and on to non-white women as exotically seductive.

However, I find this perspective inadequate and reductive - leaving me with a sense of 'so what?' Presumably for psychotherapy, 'owning' or 'coming to terms with' shadow contents should remove or reduce the power of such projections. The snag is, to pursue the example I have chosen, that we are in an epoch and culture where material acquisitiveness and control of sexuality are not optional. They are facts of our social and psychological existence and so too

---

[25] Miles, R (1989), Racism, Routledge, London, p39, quoted in Gordon, P (1993), 'Souls in Armour; Thoughts on Psychoanalysis and Racism', British Journal of Psychotherapy, **10**, 1.
[26] Jung, CW 16, para 470; CW 11, para 131.
[27] Samuels, A, Shorter B, Plaut, F (eds.) (1986), A Critical Dictionary of Jungian Analysis, Routledge, London, p. 139.

are the projections that go with them. It is also no accident that there are groups available to receive such projections. The history that makes one, also made the other.

The trouble with theorising with the shadow is that we get seduced by the ego-shadow split. Jung was aware of this when he emphasised: 'the essential thing is not the shadow but the body which casts it', and also that: 'les extremes se touchent ... Our mistake lies in supposing that the radiant things are done away with by being explained from the shadow side'.[28] In other words, substance and shadow are two indivisible aspects of a single phenomena. They co-exist in such a way that from the point of view of shadow theorising, the prospect for change looks pessimistic.

I need now to call back the self-other paradigm and hold it up, as it were, like a transparency through which to view Shadow theorising and the theory of Opposites. What is immediately noticeable as a difference between the Shadow theory and Opposites theory is that, in the former, the Other is necessarily rejected and negatively valued to preserve the superiority and 'rightness' of the self. But in the theory of Opposites the two sides are sustained in ambivalence, the tension of the contradiction is tolerated. When tolerance of this ambivalence breaks down a split occurs and I am maintaining that Shadow theorising only accounts for this moment, namely the splitting. For a deeper explanation of self and other, and racism, historically and psychologically, we need to pursue the theory of the Opposites.

The Opposites

In *The Political Psyche*, Andrew Samuels recommends a wariness of 'excessive dependence on complementarity, on the dogma of 'the opposites', on oppositional thinking, and, above all, on essentialism'.[29] He states:

> 'It is not enough to simply accept or reject 'the opposites'. We have to try and make a psychological theory about them so as to explain their immense psychopolitical power.

---

[28] Jung, CW 16, para 145; CW 16, para 146.
[29] Samuels, A (1993), The Political Psyche, Routledge, London, p. 329.

Racism, Incest and Modernity

> We have to try to explain how opposites such as Jew/German, homosexual/heterosexual, black/white, female/male, thinking/feeling actually work on the cultural level. What kind of profound split in humanity and human ideation is being carried by these opposites?.....If we make a psychological theory that explains some of these political issues, then we might be better placed to examine, and dispute, what is really meant by 'marginal' '.[30]

Jung maintained 'the opposites are the ineradicable and indispensable preconditions of all psychic life'.[31] By definition, a theory of opposites refers to opposing, irreconcilable forces co-existing in the psyche or the Jungian self (that is, the whole conscious-unconscious mind). There is a sense here of an opposition similar to the 'self and other' I have been referring to, but in this formulation it is located within the self. As I have said, the idea of the shadow is attractive to an analysis of racism because racism always involves defining the Other as inferior, and thus helps to achieve (affectually and politically) the unambivalent definition of a 'superior' self. But viewed from the perspective of a theory of opposites, it may be said that by splitting off parts of the self and projecting them onto a perceived Other, as happens in racism, what occurs is not so much a defining of self and other, but a denying of the self - by which I mean a denial in the sense of the self's potential for fuller, deeper, psychological experience through *dialogue with itself*. This is epitomised by the dialogue, or intercourse or *conjunctio*, between the conscious mind and the unconscious. From the point of view of the self this intercourse is a meeting of like with like. Contradictorily, to the conscious mind it is also a potentially threatening collision of opposites.

The Incest Symbol

I will now expand on these ideas by examining the relationship between racism, the Incest symbol in Jung, the belief in cannibalism in history and the role of marginality in late modernity.

---

[30] Samuels, A, The Political Psyche, pp. 329-330.
[31] Jung, CW 14, para 206.

Teaching Transference

Where I chose the word 'dialogue' above, Jung uses the word 'union' as he points out how

> 'Incest symbolises union with one's own being, it means individuation or becoming a self ... Incest is simply the union of like with like.'.[32]

Incest, on one level a concrete social possibility subject to a universal taboo, is also, on another level, a nurturing symbol of inner communication. Incest appears to qualify as occupying both the 'external' social-cultural sphere and the 'internal' psychological sphere. Jung cites Layard's anthropological work on tribal groups where social practices organise the group into two lineage halves. By organising marriage between the cross-cousins of the two lineages, the benefits of both endogamy and exogamy are retained. This is cited as evidence of social organisation responding to the incest instinct; and not only does the social group achieve the closest marriage system short of incest itself, but what Jung emphasises in Layard is that:

> 'He regards the endogamous (incest) tendency as a genuine instinct which if denied realisation in the flesh, must realise itself in the spirit. Just as the exogamous order made culture possible in the first place, so also it contains a latent spiritual purpose'.[33]

Jung then explains how with the expansion of population, the exogamous system advances while the endogamous tendency is repressed. The concrete lived social form is only possible with its psychological counterbalance:

'The conscious personality with its one-track (exogamous) tendency comes up against an invisible (endogamous) opponent, and because this is unconscious it is felt to be a stranger and therefore manifests itself in a projected form'.[34]

(It is important to note at this point that the shadow is far from being the only 'stranger' who is 'projected'.) Historically, Jung suggests, it makes its appearance first in human figures - political leaders, kings and queens who 'have have the power to do what others

---

[32] Jung, CW 16, para 419.
[33] Jung, CW 16 para 458.
[34] Jung, CW 16, para 438.

may not do', but it shifted to the sphere of the gods (as this was the source of kingly power):

> 'The endogamous tendency finds an outlet in the exalted sphere of the gods and in the higher world of the spirit'[35]

he writes, thus providing a neat Jungian looping of psyche's beginnings in instinctive forces and the life of the spirit on the highest level.

But what happens in the historical case of cultural developments that, firstly, deny the link between rulers and the gods (in other words, deny the 'divine right of kings') and then de-link human purpose from the 'will' of a creator God? This, of course, is exactly what occurred in the epoch under scrutiny. The Christian church, corrupted by its own secular materiality and no longer a viable container for the spirit, could not supply a cultural form for the projection Jung describes.

To summarise, modern discourse on racism focuses on the Other, but the apparent hatred and rejection of the Other can be viewed as a refusal or inability to proceed further in spiritual and psychological growth - an opting for the 'cult of consciousness'. Ironically, the Other perceived in the racially differentiated can be viewed as an alikeness, a projected property of the self that when encountered under particular cultural and individual psychological conditions strikes chords of incestuous possibilities and a fear of the depth and danger, and a loss of the material world, which personal spiritual advance could entail.

Incest and Cannibalism

I have already mentioned the Jung-Layard theory of the incest instinct being projected as a prerogative of the gods. Alongside this, cannibalism has also been regarded as the gods' prerogative and is found in Greek and other myths. Marina Warner maintains that, 'incest figures as a form of metaphorical cannibalism: eating

---

[35] Jung, CW 16, para 439.

your own'[36], the link being, again, the union of like with like. Warner does not explore the depth psychological implications of this but her paper as a whole is very useful for the links I am making between racism, incest and modernity. Cannibalism as an image can be viewed as part of the same problem that the incest symbol carries; at one level this is the tension of the endogamy/exogamy position, and at a further level the tension of the Opposites - centrally, the conscious-unconscious processes in the self. At the same time it is a material belief central to the racism of this epoch. Let me illustrate. On his first sighting of the Indies on Columbus's second voyage, Coma, on board with Columbus writes, 'These islands are inhabited by Canabilli, a wild unconquered race which feeds on human flesh. I would be right to call them anthropophagi'.[37] For centuries Europe had heard about strange tribes of man eaters. Seen as violators of the Lord's natural law by which 'higher' orders were expected to eat only 'lower' ones, the anthropophagi were in the forefont of a pantheon of monsters. So when Columbus understood from his friendly Taino Indians that there was a fierce tribe of Caribas (the name from which, all over Europe, we get Canibas then cannibal) in other islands, he encouraged the myth of the cannibal. As Sale says,

> 'Whenever the people of an island were....non-hostile, the Spanish declared that they were the Tainos.... and whenever they were deemed to be hostile, or at least defensive, they were said to be the warlike Carib, the bad Indians.'[38]

The myth, from being originally imposed by the Europeans, then becomes embedded in subsequent European chronicles and history. Anthropological evidence shows there has been no adequate documentation of cannibalism as a custom in any society, including 'the very aborigines who name now means man-eaters'[39] The clue to the meaning of the belief in cannibals lies in the discourse of the Other, in this case the Savage Beast.

> 'Reports of cannibalism provided the means of justifying the enslavement and deportation of these creatures so

---

[36] Warner, M (1994), 'Beautiful Beasts', The Independent.
[37] Sale, K, The Conquest of Paradise, p. 129.
[38] Sale, K, The Conquest of Paradise, p. 131.
[39] Quoted in Sale, K, The Conquest of Paradise, p. 133.

Racism, Incest and Modernity

> clearly beyond the pale of God's favour that they could rightly be regarded as beasts,....the myth...permitted the denigration, and thus the conquest and exploitation, of peoples whose lands were seen as increasingly desirable in European eyes.'[40]

This is surely no shadow projection here, but points to a more fundamental split in the psyche where, having begun to loosen ties to God and Church, the European psyche can itself behave like God in *recreating man*. Only through European man himself, and not God through His Church, denoting the human and the non-human, the bestial Other, and thereby his own world order, could the psychological conditions for European expansion be laid. Marina Warner points out how the cannibal myth is often reinforced with 'they eat their own children' which again superimposes incest and cannibalism and underlines a connection which is both psychological and cultural. This lends support to a view of a psychic split where loss of true religious forms allows a symbol to fall from the gods onto a worldly other. Moreover, the secularisation of the symbol is not a tendency subsequent to a debased culture, it is not just part of a trajectory, but is the psychological force that energises the social collective and allows a particular form of relationship with, and belief about, 'the world' to progress. The linkage between the incest symbol and the cannibal myth brings home the linkage between racism and the failure of psychic intercourse or union in this epoch.

The Margin

Because of the dangerous ubiquity of the paradigm of self and other, we need to find a position 'outside' the essentialism of oppositional views, a position from which these very views can be addressed. We can designate this as the margin, the space off the page where critical notes and directions can be inscribed in preparation for the redrafting. As bell hooks writes, with direct reference to consciousness of racism, the margin is a site we should stay in to discover 'the possibility of radical perspective from which to see

---

[40] Sale, K, The Conquest of Paradise, pp. 134-135.

and create, to imagine alternatives, new worlds'.[41] I have difficulties with the concept of the postmodern - I sometimes feel the 'post-' pretends to a transcendence already accomplished rather than the transition we are painfully pursuing. Nevertheless, I agree with hooks when she notes how postmodern culture is particular for its ruptures and fragmentation which provides space for radical thinking, which can result in new and varied forms of bonding across groups and disciplines that have never previously been in dialogue.

> 'The overall impact of postmodernism is that many other groups now share with black folks a sense of deep alienation, despair, uncertainty, loss of sense of grounding even if it is not informed by shared circumstance. Radical postmodernism calls attention to those shared sensibilities ... '[42]

This is exactly what Samuels is referring to when he urges us to

> 'take our sense of fragmentation, fracture and complexity as healing as well as wounding to a sense of political and social empowerment'.[43]

On the same page as this he refers to depth psychology as the precursor of late 20th century resacralisation thus indicating its potential to subvert the dominant elements in the individual and the collective culture, by being able to address what is most fundamental in the psyche of modernity.

Racism especially, although it is far from alone in this, can benefit from an analysis that employs the healing potential of fragmentation and complexity by finding a site of expression in the margin, between the fragments. This approach can also serve to confuse the splitting tendencies of the paradigm of self and other through a plural approach to the fragmentation, not for the sake of a spurious, and false, wholeness, but more the value and insight to be gained through a discovery of what can be found of the fragments as they are reflected in each other.

---

[41] hooks, b (1991), Yearning: Race, Gender and Cultural Politics, Turnaround, London, p.150.
[42] hooks, b, Yearning: Race, Gender and Cultural Politics, p. 27.
[43] Samuels, A, The Political Psyche, p.11.

Racism, Incest and Modernity

As a platform for critique of the dominant culture and its products like racism, the margin is a specific site. But within texts on race and cultural politics, there is a danger that the margin can be used as a site to keep the racially other situated where their voice is silenced by the centre or dominant academic culture which says:

> 'No need to hear your voice. Only tell me about your pain. I want to know your story. And then I will tell it back to you in a new way'.[44]

It also strikes me that the worst type of psychotherapy could be similarly accused of such a distortion by its own class of 'experts', (The tendency to seek out discrete traumas from early life, such as previously 'forgotten' sexual abuse, comes to mind here). But hooks goes on to emphasise that marginality is more than a site of deprivation,

> 'it is a site of radical possibility, a space of resistance ... a central location for the production of counter-hegemonic discourse that is not just found in words but in habits and the way one lives.'[45]

Above all it is a site one should stay in to discover 'the possibility of radical perspective from which to see and create, to imagine alternatives, new worlds'.[46] This, for all its romantic idealism, is the importance of the margin - those places in society where the non-conformist, the critical, the excluded and the non-qualifying subsist, often in deprivation but with a particular advantage. In this site, the tectonic pressures that sustain a split psyche, keeping the unconscious from dialogue with consciousness, maintaining dualistic paradigms and divisive ideation, are at their weakest. I am reminded in this of Andrew Samuel's views in *The Political Psyche*. He also emphasises the creative potential for the resacralisation of culture which stems from the margins; these may be, in the fields of gender and the family, the challenges to essentialist assumptions that single parent families and lesbian mothers provide, but Samuels also ranges as far as suggesting the psychological potential in

---

[44] hooks, b, Yearning: Race, Gender and Cultural Politics, p. 152.
[45] hooks, b, Yearning: Race, Gender and Cultural Politics, p. 149.
[46] hooks, b, Yearning: Race, Gender and Cultural Politics, p. 150.

his global idea of a 'poor politics'.⁴⁷ Economically and politically other pressures are certainly on for these groups, but importantly, perhaps the psychological pressure to conform to a split, Other-sustaining existence is off.

But finally a warning: in using the concept of the margin we need to be careful with our boundaries in modern life. The white working class racist, employed or unemployed might, from some narrow economic or political point of view be deemed marginal. But his very failure to recognise the racially other as anything but inferior, despised and Other, are his very qualifications for membership of the centre. He overrides and undermines his potential for powerful marginality - as one of those exploited by the dominant economic system - by psychologically and emotionally investing energy instead in his maintenance and hatred of an Other. His split state remains intact and he persists in a static class position, unconsciously identified with his own oppression.

Modernity: The Conclusion?

The span of modernity over the last five hundred years is coterminous with the dis-integrating of psyche, beginning with the material-spiritual splits in culture and politics, and then within the economics, philosophy and science of these centuries. This has been developed and reproduced through succeeding forms: mechanisation and the advance of industrialisation, and later the globe-shrinking power of air and space travel and the revolution in communications that information technology has produced.

For Jung, these conditions of modernity, 'increasing internationalism and the weakening of religion', have resulted in the modern phenomenon of the mass-man for which there is

> 'but one remedy: the inner consolidation of the individual, who is otherwise threatened with inevitable stultification and dissolution in the mass psyche.'⁴⁸

---

⁴⁷ Samuels, A, The Political Psyche.
⁴⁸ Jung, CW 16, para 443; Jung, CW 16, para 443.

Racism, Incest and Modernity

Marshall Berman's description of modernity from the sociological point of view, would ring true at every stage of the epoch:

> 'To be modern is to find ourselves in an environment that promises us adventure, power, joy, growth, transformation of ourselves and the world and, at the same time, that threatens to destroy everything we have, everything we know, everything we are.'[49]

I use this statement to introduce the psychologist Stephen Frosh's view that within the racist psyche is a

> 'repudiation of modernity, of multiplicity and heterogeneity. Racist ideology is the building of a fort....to defend....the integrity of the disintegrated self.'[50]

What is of note in this point of view is the emphasis on racism as a 'fort' - that is, a defence. I am in disagreement with this in that my own emphasis is on racism as an attack. Rather than a defence against fragmentation, it is an attack on the conjunctio, an attack on the potentially healing dialogue within the psyche. Frosh's view seems to rely on the sense of a missing homogeneity, a Freudian homeostasis producing an image of an all white 'golden age' in the racist psyche, that racism is defending itself against and trying to preserve or rather, restore. I prefer the view that such 'wholeness', to use an inadequate word, has to be actively achieved. It seems to me that overcoming fragmentation is the process of individuation where fragmentation is worked on as the psyche develops through inner dialogue and the linking of fragmented parts. Modernity, as a psychological mode, requires a split psyche, it requires an Other to be the object of its instrumentality . Therefore, I favour viewing racism as an integral element in the split sustaining process. By becoming conscious of this aspect of its function we may be able to address it, but only side by side with addressing similar functions that sustain our condition.

When reading Jung on the psyche and society we should note Peter Homan's analysis of Jung in the context of modernity when he reminds us that 'Jung rendered normative a lack of meaning in the social sphere' and, 'In the world of Jung's thought, the mind

---

[49] Berman, Marshall (1982), All That Is Solid Melts Into Air, Verso, London, p. 15.
[50] Frosh, S, 'Psychoanalysis and Racism', p. 233.

became society and church - a world within a world'.⁵¹ This warns us that Jung, like psychoanalysis, tended not to stand in the two places of the social and the psychological but collapsed them in his thought into one. However, this also demonstrates the point that modernity, with its inadequate spiritual forms and emphasis on materiality and instrumental-rationality, requires such a collapse, and the eventual transcendence of it. Jung's emphasis on symbolic forms, like incest, contribute to 'demodernisation' as Homans understands it by which he means a challenge to modernity, and a resistance from the margin. ⁵²This reminds us that, despite a degree of legitimisation of depth psychology achieved through alliances with medicine and other establishment disciplines, depth psychology, because of its attention to unconscious processes, will always speak from the margin. Possession of such a voice from the margin enables the critique of modernity depth psychology can, and should, offer in the service of healing.

The unsatisfactoriness of modern mass life and the trend towards the narcissistic that Homans and others have noted in recent times provide a context for the popularity of ideas of turning inward for healing and individuation that are associated with Jungian theory and therapy. But we cannot eschew the social order for too long individuation, the healing of a split soul, needs institutionalising in the social and political order to produce the healing of split worlds and the dissolving of modernity's worst effects such as racism. When Marx said of modern times that 'All that is solid melts into air' he failed to add that the most insidious elements have the highest melting point.

This paper does not pretend to offer any prescription for undoing racism. On the contrary, I have pointed out, rather pessimistically perhaps, its embeddedness in the psyche and culture via material practices supported by conscious attitudes, themselves based on unconscious splits in the psyche: the failure of the dialogue or conjunctio between the conscious and the unconscious mind.

Racism is only one example of many phenomena developed by such psychological and cultural shifts, 'otherness' according to gender being the second major form that comes to mind. So this

---

⁵¹ Homans, P, Jung in Context; Modernity and the Making of a Psychology, p. 200; p. 201.
⁵² Homans, Jung in Context, p. 204.

paper has been rather a global overview of a state of mind and culture that produces such splits. As I have mentioned, any change in racism would have to go hand in hand with change in parallel effects of modernity, delivering a new existential attitude based on transcendence and transformation of the split psyche. For psychotherapy, this could amount to a powerful and transforming attitude and movement that gives lived meaning to the proposition that 'In healing the patient, you heal the culture'.

From the Pleasure of Power to the Power of Pleasure: Popular culture in search of a new identity

Milena Kirova

In 1924 a book was published in the Soviet Union - one among many - by an author called Zalkind: The Revolution and the Young People. It contained twelve Commandments to the young people, regulating their sexual behaviour. Commandment Two read: 'Sexual desire for an object belonging to a hostile class is as perverse as sexual desire for a crocodile or an orang-utan.'

In December 1989 the first nude body for the last 45 years appeared on the front page of a Bulgarian newspaper. The name of the newspaper was Patriot and the body belonged to an American female model.

There exists a vast space of Desire between the Pleasure to Command society and the Pleasure to feel commanded by instincts; that is between political power and unrepressed sexuality. This space in Eastern Europe is now being quickly occupied by popular culture, flourishing for the last two years. Popular culture spreads over a vast range of works: starting with erotic literature and movies, ending with works of elite culture accepted as belonging to the popular one by mass audience (mainly from the premises of American and especially French post-modern art). There is also a campaign on behalf of many critics and historians of art to devalue popular culture, to exhibit the dangers of it. This campaign seems to be just another attempt to command society under the new conditions. It is not a matter of choice - to accept or not to accept popular culture - because as a matter of fact it is present everywhere. May be there exists a third way for the East European students of culture - to understand and explain the psychological necessity of popular culture - and also, try the pleasure of it.

We must admit that popular culture is unrivalled in its ability to generate mythological thinking - affecting the unconscious collective ideas of each society. The communist type of civilisation succeeded to build an extremely strong and well integrated system of

From the Pleasure of Power to the Power of Pleasure

mythological images - even the image of the should-not-be desired object being one of them. Here are some of these images: the laborious and honest peasant; the revolutioneer, faithful to death; the man of culture and education serving the interests of the Party - these on the one side; and on the other, the corrupt bourgeois businessman; the western prostitute; the vicious and cunning CIA spy. Then the level of mythical institutions, whose function was protected by an information taboo, came: The Party, the Congress of the Party, the Central Committee of the Party and so on. At the very top of the mythological pyramid irresistibly symbolic images were situated, coinciding with archetypes of magic or religious origin: the red star (it corresponds to the Nazi swastika), the temple (sacred buildings and especially mausoleums), the Supreme Father (usually the general secretary of the Party or some of the first Communist leaders), the Holy Trinity (the icons of Marx, Engels and Lenin, hanging everywhere), the Second Paradise, the fraternity of all people (the idea of internationalism), the rebellion of the proletarian brothers against the power of Father-Capital.

The Communist Society grew up living and thinking upon collective ideas of mythological origin. People were not supposed and were not used to construct ideas of their own. I would give an example in Bulgarian context. Among the most popular, written in all textbooks of History and known by everybody slogans of Communist ideology was a statement of Georgi Dimitrov before the Leipzig Trial:

> 'The wheel of History is turning and it won't stop turning on until the final victory of Communism.'

There is an obvious logical mistake in this statement which makes it anti-historical, anti-dialectical. What will happen after the final victory of Communism, when the wheel of History will stop turning? The end of History? Nobody ever thought of this obvious mistake but just kept repeating it for years.

Communist society did not exist upon a rational psychological basis which made it strong in a special way. Communist civilisation developed a very deep attitude towards collective and popular models of thinking and feeling. Communist culture as a whole was a kind of popular culture.

The 1989 came. A vast gap appeared, an existential and semiotic gap. The old meanings turned meaningless. The old myths didn't work any more, there were no new myths available yet. The audience, deeply shaken in its social and cultural faith, tried to fill up the semiotic gap with new ready-made patterns. These patterns had to be borrowed from abroad because of the total devaluation of the only cultural system available - the Communist one. The people of Eastern Europe needed new collective ideas and mythological images. Naturally enough, they quickly found them in foreign popular culture. The contents were different, even more attractive, but the psychological principle of immediate irrational group identification was the same.

The collapse of the Communist order seems to have begun destroying the very roots of the social and cultural identity of East European people. Reception of and adaptation to foreign popular culture offers an easier and undoubtedly a more pleasurable way to new identity, especially as far as societies made unable to generate their own existential patterns are concerned. Foreign popular discourses help turn the process of cultural destruction into a process of cultural deconstruction.

Here come two other sets of questions:

The first is concentrated around the problems: How long is this process is going to be helpful, is it possible to prevent the obvious dangers of it or is there some perceptible boundary between pseudo-identity and authentic national identity. I don't dare to answer these questions right now, it is too early.

The second group of problems leads us in another direction: Which foreign culture/cultures and which other identity/identities are being predominantly borrowed? Now I shall speak of Bulgaria only because it is the situation I really know. During the last two years we have undergone a sweeping wave of desire for being American. American popular culture has invaded our life: we listen to VOA Europe, we read Mario Puzo and Thomas Harris, we watch Kim Basinger and Arny Schwarzenegger, we eat American burgers and dream American dreams. And it is the same not only in the sphere of culture but also of economics and social life. Americanisation has become a touchstone for the very desire to change, to forget the disgrace of the past, to find a non Communist identity. The invasion of American culture is not a problem specific for Bulgaria only. It is a problem I suppose for many other European and Asian countries, either 'peripheral' or 'central'. But there is something which I find special for Bulgaria. The desire for

From the Pleasure of Power to the Power of Pleasure

American identity is so profound, so comprehensive that there is only one historic phenomenon it can be compared with: the invasion of Soviet culture half a century ago. The two phenomena seem to be the opposite, deeply interrelated sides of one and the same process, one and the same historical attitude. They spring from a complex of national inferiority and try to compensate for it by identification with the institution of highest political power and authority of the moment.

The traditions of Bulgarian culture and history have established a type of national identity very different from the American style of living and thinking. It is this difference now which seduces the post-totalitarian society of Bulgaria. It helps society to create an illusion that the past is gone, that the past has been a matter of a false ideology, bad economics and corrupt politics but not a matter of voluntary personal choice and collective compliant attitude. The unimpeded reception of American popular culture resembles the changing of costumes between two acts of a play. Behind the scene of their consciousness, of their own unchangeable identity grown up people are looking for another face, for another role in life and it is not strange that they put on the most fashionable, bright and eccentric clothes available - the clothes of American popular culture. It was only two years ago that this culture was officially devalued, rejected, even banned. This helped it turn in the minds of the people into something different, desirable - something Other than what they were. The thirst for American (popular) identity nowadays has a tinge of political meaning - it stands symbolically for the desire of everyone to be the person he was not (allowed to be) yesterday.

There is also something masochistic in this desire to lose identity. It seems that behind the curtains of pleasure and entertainment the post-totalitarian society wants to punish itself for being too submissive and compliant. It is strange that the act of punishment once again repeats the act of crime?

Another aspect of the desire to look for new social features is represented by the possibility to identify with cultural patterns of small difference. For Bulgarians and in the thematic space of my subject it means reception of popular culture coming from other ex-Communist or Balkan countries - that is from the Eastern and Southern peripheries of European civilisation. A paradox easily discernible and can be defined as follows: the smaller the difference of cultural patterns, the bigger the reluctance to identify with them. As far as the other East European countries are concerned, the explanation seems to be pretty simple. Communist culture everywhere was of one kind and very much alike. National differences and traditions tended to dissolve under the pressure of ideological visions and typical images. Communist society was supposed to have headed for the Second Paradise. As we all know, there are no nationalities, no historic traditions and no specific differences among the people in Paradise.

Leo Tolstoy had written in the beginning of his famous novel Anna Karenina: 'All happy families look alike, each unhappy family is unhappy in its own way'. Communist society of the future would resemble a congregation of happy denationalised families. That is why now not only popular but even most serious culture coming from East European countries is totally neglected, profoundly undesired, practically unsalable. Instead of sharing their common problems, finding together new ways to democratic identity, the post-totalitarian peoples of different countries don't respect each other, don't pay attention to the achievements of their cultures and make their best to forget the common past as quickly as possible.

At the beginning of this century Freud coined a concept, having in mind the negative attitude of West Europeans towards their own Jewish population - narcissism of the small differences.

Nowadays we see the same old phenomenon, only slightly altered. Another 'Bulgarian' example contributes to the clarification of the problem. Never before the traditions and the recent achievements of Greek, or Turkish, or Serbian culture - the Balkan type of civilisations a whole - have been so totally neglected and frankly underestimated. It seems that the only function of these cultures now is to serve as a transmission between Bulgarian and some central, mainly American, patterns of popular art. It is clear enough that the people of Bulgarian, more than ever, do not want to see themselves as they really are, and try to escape the unbearable freedom of realistic self-assessment. What is more - even the students of culture do not see, or do not want to see and discuss in public the importance of these socio-cultural phenomena. Among the many reasons I would like to designate the general attitude of disbelief in words.

From the Pleasure of Power to the Power of Pleasure

The inflation of verbal discourse was one of the most typical features of East European totalitarian society. The words tended to lose their denotative meanings and to function mainly by the secondary meanings which they got in a highly ideologized cultural context. Let us remember the statement of Georgi Dimitrov which I quoted. This devaluation of words and original meanings generated suspicion, sometimes even aversion, towards verbal texts and especially towards those of them which created their own, idiosyncratic fields of secondary meanings. Undoubtedly the broadest semiotic gap in the post-totalitarian society appeared in the space of verbal discourse. This is one of the reasons which have made recent Bulgarian literature undesired and practically unavailable on the market for the last two years(besides the unbearable competition with foreign texts, the death of the old author and so on).

This takes us away once again to the desire for popular culture, because popular culture does not rely upon a complex interplay of secondary meanings, it is not interested in the ideological context of a certain civilisation. Popular art affects the unconscious primal ideas and patterns of experience, it is a way to depersonalisation, creating a common body of pleasure for the individuals, tired of indoctrination and alienation. Popular culture then is a way to live without words - at least until the moment comes when the words will stop symbolising slogans and ideological dogmas, 'eternal' and 'ultimate' truths.

Index

A

Academic freedom, 11
Academic settings, 1, 12
Adorno, T W, 141, 163
Agnew, J, 91
Ambivalence, 17, 172
Analysis, 19, 27, 28, 29, 30, 31, 32, 34, 35, 37, 38, 39, 41, 42, 44, 46, 52, 56, 57, 69, 81, 84, 85, 86, 87, 88, 114, 115, 125, 127, 130, 137, 146
Analysis, analysts, 3, 11, 19, 21, 25, 29, 30, 31, 32, 34, 35, 38, 39, 41, 42, 48, 49, 52, 53, 55, 63, 69, 70, 71, 72, 79, 81, 84, 86, 87, 88, 90, 92, 98, 99, 101, 103, 104, 105, 106, 110, 114, 115, 123, 125, 126, 130, 134, 136, 138, 146, 159, 161, 162, 163, 164, 165, 166, 167, 173, 178, 181
Analysts. See also Psychotherapists, 9, 23, 52, 71, 72, 86
Analytical psychology, 22, 185
Analytical Psychology (see also Jung), 15, 16, 17, 18, 22, 23, 24, 25, 90
Jungian Studies), 15, 16, 18, 20, 21, 23, 24
Anxiety, anxieties, 48, 58, 65, 81, 98, 102, 104, 105, 107, 108, 111
Art history, 55
Authoritarianism, 74
Authority, 74, 155, 187

B

Balint, Michael, 22, 85
Banister, D, 91
Bargrave family, 145, 147, 148, 149, 150, 151, 152, 153, 154, 155, 156, 157
Beethoven, Ludwig van, 142
Berman, Marshall, 181
Bion, Wilfred, 23, 40, 50, 51, 53, 56, 57, 58
Borromean knot, 124, 130, 131, 133
Britain, 1, 2, 9, 11, 12, 13, 15, 21, 22, 23, 33, 44, 45, 52, 55, 56, 93, 99, 104, 116, 133, 137, 142, 147, 148, 149, 150, 154, 160, 171
British Psychological Society, 23
Brown, R, 92
Bulgaria, 184, 185, 186, 187, 188, 189

C

Cannibal, cannibalism, 176, 177
Citizens, citizenship. See also Politics, 24
Clinic, 1, 2, 3, 4, 9, 10, 11, 12, 13, 15, 17, 19, 20, 21, 22, 29, 30, 44, 45, 54, 55, 57, 58, 67, 72, 88, 101, 115, 119
Clinic, clinical, 20
Clinic, clinicians, 3, 5, 9, 20, 22, 44
Collections, collecting, 136, 145, 146, 147, 148, 150, 151, 152, 154, 155, 156

Index

Columbus, Christopher, 168, 176
Communism (see also Socialism), 185, 186, 187, 188
Competition, 18, 21, 62, 189
Controversy, 12, 18, 24, 25, 60, 120, 173
Counsellor, 10
Cult, 19, 146, 175
Culture, 4, 17, 21, 25, 45, 46, 55, 58, 61, 68, 71, 72, 73, 74, 80, 84, 85, 88, 89, 99, 101, 136, 139, 141, 146, 155, 160, 161, 162, 164, 165, 166, 167, 170, 171, 173, 174, 175, 177, 178, 179, 180, 182, 184, 185, 186, 187, 188, 189
Cure. See also Treatment, 10, 27, 29

D

Declaration of Independence, American, 170
Defence, 37, 70, 86, 136, 138, 164, 176, 181
Depth psychology, 18, 58, 71, 161, 166, 178, 182
Dimitrov, Georgi, 185, 189
Disciples, 87
Discourse, 2, 25, 33, 34, 35, 37, 38, 42, 43, 58, 70, 71, 73, 74, 75, 82, 135, 141, 143, 159, 161, 171, 175, 176, 179, 186, 189
Disposition, 95
Dogmatism, dogma, 46, 69, 80, 81, 87, 88, 96, 172

E

Eastern Europe, 184, 186, 188, 189
Education, 10
Ego psychology, 81

Eire, 9
Enlightenment, 27, 29, 31, 127, 130, 168
Envy, 18, 58
Erikson, Erik, 86
Ethics, 18, 41, 44, 82
Ethnicity, 22, 25, 87, 162
Existential approaches, 23, 82, 183, 185, 186
Expectation, 10, 12, 21, 95, 96, 137

F

Fanon, Franz, 160, 162, 164, 165
Fantasy, 10, 25, 28, 31, 48, 53, 86, 102, 118, 119
Ferenczi, Sandor, 4, 63, 67, 81
Film Studies, 13, 45
Fordham, Michael, 18, 94
Frame of the analytic session, 22
France, 11, 22, 37, 116, 119, 133, 184
Frantz, R L, 91
Freud, Sigmund, 1, 17, 18, 22, 27, 28, 29, 30, 31, 32, 33, 37, 39, 41, 47, 48, 49, 50, 51, 52, 57, 63, 64, 67, 71, 79, 82, 84, 85, 86, 88, 90, 98, 99, 101, 102, 103, 104, 105, 106, 107, 108, 109, 111, 112, 117, 118, 122, 123, 125, 126, 127, 128, 133, 145, 146, 165, 188
Frosh, Stephen, 164, 165, 181

G

Gender, 13, 25, 92, 160, 178, 179
German Society for Analytical Psychology, 24
Germany, 24, 99, 100, 173
Glover, Edward, 85
God, 28, 168, 170, 175, 177

Graf, Hans ('Little Hans'), 100
Graf, Max, 99, 100, 102, 106, 112
Greed, 169, 171
Groups, 23

H

Heidegger, Martin, 19, 60, 64, 99, 119
Higher Education Research and Information Network in Psychoanalysis, The (THERIP), 3
Hillman, James, 18
Historical approaches, 23
history of science, 19
Horkheimer, Max, 62
Hudson, Liam, 17
Humanistic approaches, 23, 84
Hysteria, hysteric, 33, 34, 43, 48

I

Identity. See also Self, 28, 40, 90, 148, 162, 184, 186, 187, 188
Ideology, ideological, 21, 46, 73, 120, 149, 153, 154, 166, 181, 185, 187, 188, 189
Il Trovatore, 103
Imago, 85, 118, 119, 120, 121, 122, 123, 124
Incest, 159, 161, 173, 174, 175, 177, 182
Infancy, 28, 53, 54, 55, 58, 86, 90, 91, 92, 93, 95, 116, 117, 166
interdisciplinarity, multidisciplinarity, 1, 2, 5, 12
Interpretation, 30, 85, 101, 112, 114, 115, 150

J

Jones, Ernest, 104, 113, 126, 149, 150
Joyce, James, 128, 129, 130, 131, 132, 133, 134
Jung, C G (see also Jungian Studies, Analytical Psychology), 16, 17, 18, 19, 22, 23, 24, 25, 85, 90, 94, 95, 119, 134, 161, 167, 170, 171, 172, 173, 174, 175, 180, 181, 182
Jungian Studies (see also Analytical Psychology), 15, 16

K

Klein, Melanie, 16, 23, 39, 47, 52, 53, 119, 120, 121, 122
Knowledge, 3, 15, 27, 28, 29, 30, 31, 32, 34, 35, 37, 38, 39, 42, 44, 47, 54, 55, 56, 57, 59, 61, 62, 65, 66, 68, 69, 71, 72, 73, 74, 81, 85, 86, 88, 91, 92, 93, 95, 115, 120, 132, 137, 150
Kovel, Joel, 162, 164

L

Lacan, Jacques, 16, 31, 33, 34, 35, 37, 39, 40, 41, 70, 88, 102, 104, 105, 107, 108, 109, 110, 111, 113, 115, 116, 117, 118, 119, 120, 121, 122, 123, 124, 125, 127, 128, 129, 130, 131, 132, 133, 134
Laplanche, Jean, 23, 119
Leaders, leadership. See also Politics, Authoritarianism, 18, 24
Literature, criticism, 24

Index

M

Mannoni, O, 164
Marx, Karl, 165, 182, 185
Mastery, 12, 30, 33, 34, 40, 70, 74, 80, 117, 118, 119, 130, 148
Medical insurance, 10
Mirrors, mirroring, 58, 61, 80, 85, 92, 116, 117, 125
Models, modelling, 24, 54, 55, 56, 57, 58, 70, 80, 153, 185
Modernism, modernity, 65, 130, 159, 161, 162, 163, 164, 165, 168, 170, 176, 178, 180, 181, 182, 183
Morality, 18, 135, 168
Museums, 145, 146, 156
Music, 99, 100, 135, 136, 137, 138, 139, 141, 142, 143, 144
Mysticism, 17, 19, 49, 97

N

Nachträglichkeit, 117, 123
Narcissism, 45, 48, 50, 51, 52, 53, 54, 56, 57, 58, 65, 122, 140, 142, 182, 188
Nature, 5, 21, 23, 24, 46, 48, 50, 51, 53, 64, 66, 67, 72, 94, 106, 112, 116, 123, 138, 140, 142, 143, 168, 169, 170, 176
Nazism, 17, 18, 185
New York Psychoanalytic Society, 79

O

Object Relations School (see also Klein, Melanie), 12, 22, 23, 45, 105, 113, 166
Occult, occultism, 17
Oedipus complex, 105

Opposites, Theory of, 170, 172, 176
Origen, 81

P

Pasteur, Louis, 90
Pathologization, 10
Pathology, 85, 130
Penfield, W, 95
philosophy of science, 46
Phobia, 98, 99, 102, 103, 104, 105, 106, 108, 111, 112
Politics, 5, 19, 24, 54, 55, 58, 82, 83, 154, 155, 160, 161, 162, 164, 165, 167, 168, 170, 173, 174, 178, 179, 180, 182, 184, 187
Popper, Karl, 60, 93, 96
Postgraduate study, 1, 3, 9, 12, 13, 16, 79
Postmodernism, 19, 178
Power, 18, 61, 65, 68, 70, 74, 87, 101, 102, 122, 154, 155, 161, 164, 168, 170, 171, 174, 180, 181, 184, 185, 187
Profession, professional, 13, 18, 23, 24, 39, 153, 163
Projection, 49, 141, 143, 163, 171, 175, 177
Projective identification, 53, 114, 167
Psychotherapists. See also Analysts, 12, 13, 21
Psychotherapy, clinical, 17

Q

Qualifications, 15, 29, 119, 174, 180

193

R

Racism, 159, 160, 161, 162, 163, 164, 165, 166, 167, 169, 170, 171, 172, 173, 175, 176, 177, 178, 179, 180, 181, 182
Reik, Theodor, 79, 80, 81, 82, 84, 86
Relations with other disciplines, 3, 13, 18, 19, 23, 24, 25, 46, 47, 49, 50, 52, 53, 54, 55, 59, 63, 65, 66, 71, 72, 80, 83, 84, 86, 96, 112, 126, 127, 136, 145, 147, 151, 159, 160, 164, 170, 172, 173, 176, 180, 181, 187
Religion, 13, 17, 19, 25, 63, 71, 80, 87, 135, 177, 180, 185
Representation, 92, 116, 125, 130, 163
Repression, 50, 52, 68, 127
Resacralisation of culture, 161, 179
Research, clinical, 20
Research, general, 20, 21
Research, outcome studies, 20
Russell, Bertrand, 99

S

Samuels, Andrew, 15, 17, 18, 21, 22, 58, 161, 166, 167, 171, 172, 173, 178, 180
Sartre, Jean-Paul, 90, 93, 94, 95, 119, 153, 165
Searles, Harold, 86
Secular, secularization, 19, 168, 170, 175
Seduction, 171, 172
See
  Graf, Max, 98, 99, 103, 111
Segal, Hanna, 23
Self. See also
  Identity, 90, 97

Sexuality, 22, 25, 28, 29, 31, 40, 58, 71, 171, 179, 184
Shadow, 170, 172
Siegfried (opera), 101
Situationalism, 22
Social anthropology, 13
Social work, 13
Society for Analytical Psychology, 24
Soviet Union, 184, 187
Spain, 151
Stigma, 10
Symboli, symbolization, 39, 173
symptom, 60, 98, 104, 111, 115, 119, 126, 127, 128, 130, 134

T

Tagore, Rabindranath, 81
Tests, psychological, 26
The Universities Association for Psychoanalytic Studies (UAPS), 3, 45
Theory, theorizing, 80
Therapist, 10, 28, 41, 142
Therapy, 10, 32, 41, 64, 79, 83, 84, 87, 142, 182
Totalitarianism, 187, 188, 189
Totality, 94, 122
Training Institute of the National Psychological Association for Psychoanalysis, 79
Transitional space, 88
Trauma, 10, 13, 31, 32, 132, 140, 142, 179
Treatment. See also
  Cure, 10, 13, 27, 29, 30, 31, 38, 41, 55, 63, 64
Trickster, 25
Typology, typological thinking, 22

Index

U

Unconscious, 1, 4, 10, 44, 47, 56, 69, 72, 93, 95, 98, 99, 111, 114, 115, 116, 119, 125, 126, 127, 133, 136, 141, 143, 159, 161, 163, 168, 173, 176, 179, 182, 184, 189
Unconscuious, psychoid, 24
Undergraduate study, 3, 9, 13
United Kingdom. See also Britain, Eire, 9, 73
United States of America, 1, 9, 81, 82, 88, 100, 103, 112, 113, 154, 170, 184, 186, 187, 188
Universities Association for Psychoanalytic Studies, The (UAPS), 3
Universities Psychotherapy Association (UPA), 45
University, 1, 2, 3, 4, 5, 9, 11, 12, 13, 15, 16, 17, 20, 22, 25, 34, 37, 41, 43, 44, 45, 46, 47, 53, 54, 55, 57, 58, 59, 60, 61, 62, 63, 64, 65, 67, 68, 69, 70, 71, 72, 73, 74, 75, 80, 81, 86, 88, 90, 91, 95, 96, 97, 100, 102, 119, 122, 127, 138, 143, 145, 147, 149, 151, 154, 156, 161, 163, 166
University of Essex, 2, 16
University of Kent, 1, 2, 3, 4, 5, 9, 11, 12, 16, 45, 150, 153, 154

W

Wagner, Siegfried, 100
Warner, Marina, 175, 176, 177
Winnicott, D W, 22, 23, 79, 80, 81, 82, 84, 85, 86, 88

Z

Zizek, Slavoj, 130